D1068910

THE TRIAL OF EZRA POUND

THE TRIAL OF EZRA POUND

A Documented Account of the Treason Case by the Defendant's Lawyer

JULIEN CORNELL

THE JOHN DAY COMPANY
NEW YORK

This book is dedicated to my wife

Library of Congress Catalogue Card Number 66-19537

PRINTED IN THE UNITED STATES OF AMERICA

Contents

Appendix

INTRODUCTION

After having been confined by the United States government for thirteen years on charges of treason, Ezra Pound was released from St. Elizabeths Hospital in Washington in April, 1958, his indictment was dismissed and he was allowed to return to Italy. The story of his trial, confinement and eventual release is told here, including all the relevant documentary material from my files and public records. I was Pound's lawyer.

This is an unusual story. Ezra Pound was imprisoned for thirteen years because of an alleged crime which was never proved. He was imprisoned despite the fact that he is one of the great literary figures of our time, perhaps in part because of that fact. A many-sided man, Pound did not confine himself to poetry; he indulged also in political and economic theories which he expounded over the Rome radio during World War II. Some of his broadcasts were highly critical, even contemptuous, of the policies of the United States and its allies. The indictment charged that Pound, an American citizen, in making these broadcasts committed treason by giving "aid and comfort" to the enemy. This, Pound has always vigorously denied. "The treason," he said, "was in the White House, not in Rapallo."

However that may be, one fact clearly emerges. When he arrived in Washington jail Pound was an old man, tired and sick, unable to understand his predicament sufficiently well to defend himself. For this reason, he was adjudged unfit to be tried and was eventually released.

People will soon forget, if they have not already forgotten, the war-born passions which brought Ezra Pound to the courtroom, but they will forever remember his verse and will want to know why and how he came to be imprisoned for his utterances. Hence this book.

JULIEN CORNELL

I

THE BROADCASTS

As the war in Europe was drawing to a close, I sat in a listening booth in the office of the British Information Service in New York City listening to recordings of several of Pound's broadcasts as monitored in London. At the opening of each broadcast, an announcer made the following statement:

> "The Italian radio acting in accordance with the Fascist policy of intellectual freedom and free expression of opinion by those who are qualified to hold it, following the tradition of Italian hospitality, has offered Dr. Ezra Pound the use of the microphone twice a week. It is understood that he will not be asked to say anything whatsoever that goes against his conscience, or anything incompatible with his duties as a citizen of the United States of America."

Then I heard the voice of Ezra Pound, speaking in the folksy drawl of a plainsman from the Western United States. This was not Pound's usual manner of speech, but was affected by him for the purpose of the broadcasts. With his keen ear for language, Pound was a wonderful mimic, able to imitate to perfection the sort of speech which he probably assumed would appeal to the average listener.

The broadcasts did not sound treasonable to me. The crime of treason is defined in the Constitution as the levying of war against the United States or adhering to their enemies, giving them aid and comfort. There was no criticism of the allied war effort in the broadcasts; nothing was said to discourage or disturb American soldiers or their families. Pound's main concern was with usury and other economic sins which he conceived were being committed by an international conspiracy of Jewish bankers who were the powers behind the throne in England and had succeeded in duping the government of the United States. The broadcasts were in essence lectures in history and political and economic theory, highly critical of the course of American government beginning with Alexander Hamilton, who Pound believed started the country down the road to financial ruin. The American people were told that they did not understand what was going on in Europe and if they did, the war would not have been necessary.

It was Pound himself who had insisted that the Italian radio authorities begin the broadcasts with the statement quoted above explaining that everything which he was saying was said of his own free will. There is no doubt that his speeches were his own. No Italian propagandist would have been capable of writing them.

I never knew of anyone who heard these broadcasts over the radio, although they were received and monitored in the United States. As a radio figure, Pound did not command the interest of Lord Haw Haw, Axis Sally or Tokyo Rose. He was not an entertainer and apparently did not care whether anyone listened to him or not. It seems most unlikely that those who did hear him could have lost any affection for the United States or its war effort. It is also unlikely that any jury would reach the conclusion that the broadcasts gave "aid and comfort to the enemy" or that Pound was doing anything but exercising the good old American prerogative of criticizing his government including even President Roosevelt.

The criticism was scurrilous and vituperative. It reminded me of the way Wall Street bankers and lawyers used to talk about "that scalawag in the White House" during the early days of the New Deal.

There was a rumor that the Italian radio officials eventually cut him off the air because they were afraid that he was giving information to the allies in some sort of a code. Of course, this was not true, but Pound's strange mixture of historical and economic ideas did have a cryptic sound to it.

The indictment specifically mentions certain of the broadcasts (presumably because witnesses were available to prove that Pound made them). The government's lawyers refused to show me these broadcasts, although they planned to use them at Pound's trial. Ironically, my only information about the broadcasts came not from our own government, but from the British Information Service, which had kindly made available to me the recordings which they had on file.

Years later, after Pound's case was closed, the transcripts of his broadcasts made by the United States government became accessible at the National Archives. I obtained a complete set, but found them dreary reading. Two complete broadcasts are printed in an appendix to this book.

II

COUNSEL FOR THE DEFENSE

MY FRIEND JAMES LAUGHLIN asked me in September, 1945 if I would be willing to undertake the defense of Ezra Pound. Laughlin was Pound's publisher. He explained to me that Pound had made broadcasts over the Rome radio for which he had been indicted on charges of treason and would soon be brought to the United States for trial.

I readily agreed to look into the case, as I had always enjoyed fighting for an underdog. Much of my time in those days was spent defending the civil liberties of persons who had become entangled with the law in one way or another, such as aliens, ministers and conscientious objectors who were having difficulties with the Selective Service Law.

I told Laughlin that I was interested in taking Pound's case but would need to see him and learn more about the circumstances. Laughlin then wrote to Arthur V. Moore of Shakespear and Parkyn recommending that I be retained as counsel for the defense. Shakespear and Parkyn were solicitors for Mrs. Pound, whose maiden name was Shakespear. Moore replied:

LETTER FROM ARTHUR V. MOORE TO JAMES LAUGHLIN

London, 9th October 1945

Dear Mr. Laughlin,

Thank you for your letter of 30th September, and for your very kind assistance in suggesting Mr. Julien Cornell as Counsel for defense of our friend. I am however rather troubled with the thought that whatever his friends may think or wish to do for him, he will much prefer to conduct his defense in his own manner, and by such means as may seem expedient to him.

I have however written to him urging him to give my firm instructions to obtain the best possible Counsel, and I have advised him not to attempt to address the Court in his own defense, but to allow a lawyer experienced in Court procedure to represent his interests.

I have not received any reply to my letter, and like yourself I have no way of knowing whether it will be delivered to him. I have today however heard from Italy that correspondence with our friend is now officially permitted, and the address you should use is as follows:

MTOUSA D. T. C.*
A. P. O. 782,
U. S. ARMY
Mediterranean Theater.

Another difficulty with which I am confronted is the matter of finance. Dorothy in one of her letters to me states she is prepared to spend her last penny in the defense of her husband, but all her investments and funds in this country are in the hands of the official Custodian of Enemy Property, to whom I applied for release of funds to enable me to remit money to Dorothy for her immediate needs. I was informed by this official that release could be obtained provided I obtained confirmation from American sources in Italy that Dorothy claimed protection as an American citizen, and that there was no charge of any description filed against her personally. I asked Dorothy to obtain this, and she informs me the American Consul at Genoa has informed her her status as an American citizen has "lapsed" as she has not renewed her Passport since 1941.

I have written to the American Embassy in London for confirmation of this ruling, and expect it has been referred to Washington, D. C. for confirmation. I wonder whether Mr. McLeish could find out anything about it.

---

* Mediterranean Theatre of Operations, United States Army, Disciplinary Training Center.

Such a deprivation of citizenship would leave Dorothy a "stateless" person for she lost her British nationality on her marriage in 1914, and the officials in this country will now have no interest in her welfare until Peace is officially made with Italy, when her funds will be then released.

I am only therefore in a position to say that any fees which Mr. Cornell may charge could only be paid by Dorothy as and when her money is available, for she has ample to meet the costs, but if it will help matters I should be prepared to undertake that any costs would eventually be met, and if required I would make a personal remittance on account for this purpose.

Everything you have told me concerning Mr. Cornell is very interesting, and I am in full agreement that his services should be retained, but as I have explained I am not yet in a position to give him definite instructions until I hear from our friend that he is in agreement.

I suggest therefore that you write to him again, or alternatively when you have news of his arrival in U.S.A. that either you or McLeish should seek permission to interview him with regard to his defense, and if he agrees, then I propose we should employ a firm of American Lawyers if you think it necessary, to prepare his Case for Defense, and for them to instruct Mr. Cornell accordingly.

Several of his friends in this country are most anxious to help by stating what they know of the circumstances, and I should be prepared to send such information as is obtainable for the assistance of Mr. Cornell, or to do anything which may be of assistance from this side.

I have forwarded copies of your letter to Mr. Eliot, Mrs. Pound & Mr. Drummond.

Yours sincerely,

ARTHUR V. MOORE.

A few days later, Laughlin showed me a letter which Pound had recently written to Shakespear and Parkyn. Although Pound had been held in confinement all summer at the Military Disciplinary Center of the United States Army near Pisa, Italy, he says in his letter that his wife had not been permitted to visit him until two days previously. Here is the letter:

LETTER FROM EZRA POUND TO SHAKESPEAR AND PARKYN

5 Oct. 1945

Gentlemen:

I am very glad to get your letter of the 7th ulto: re-sent on the 24th which is the first that has reached me from the outer world, though Dorothy was permitted to visit me two days ago and brought the good news of Omar. I am very much pleased with his independence and initiative in all ways.

Also glad to observe from your stationery that John St. has not been bombed out of existence.

I am not sure that your advice is given in full knowledge of certain essential facts of my case.

For example, I was not sending axis propaganda but my own, the nucleus of which was in Brooks Adams' works 40 years ago, in Kitson's published 25 years ago, and in my own pre-war publications.

This was sent and stated to be sent at least over the medium wave, on various occasions, with the preface:

"On the principle of free expression of opinion on the part of those qualified to have an opinion, Dr. Pound has been granted the freedom of our microphone twice a week. He will not be asked to say anything contrary to his conscience or contrary to his duties as an American citizen." The twice was extended to 3 & more times. These conditions were faithfully observed by the Rome radio. I never was asked to say anything.

The investigator for the American Dept. of Justice expressed himself as convinced that I was telling him the absolute truth months ago, and has since with great care collected far more proof to that effect than I or any private lawyer could have got at.

My instinct all along has been to leave the whole matter to the U. S. Dept. of Justice, the good faith of whose agent I have had no reason to doubt.

I do not know how this will strike you, but the fantastic conditions in Italy have been such that someone who has come here and examined the facts can probably form an opinion more easily than anyone, however perspicacious at a distance.

I had hoped to see Mr. MacLeish in Washington in May while he was still in the State Dept.

You will see there are elements in the case far more interesting than my personal welfare.

I have very cordial recollections of Lloyd Stryker, he is now I believe one of the best known big lawyers in the U. S. whose fees are probably far beyond anything I could pay.

40 years ago, about 1905, when his father was President of Hamilton College, Lloyd and I must have been among his prominent headaches, Lloyd in the home, and I in the class room. BUT I should much prefer to see Mr. MacLeish before deciding on so important a step as NOT speaking on my own behalf. I believe MacLeish is himself a lawyer, and in any case he can write to me at this address. If he writes as my lawyer I would certainly be permitted to answer him as I am now answering you.

My most complete fog, my difficulty is my ABSOLUTE ignorance of what had happened in the U. S. A. and in England from 1940 to 1945.

With Mr. Dalton at the Exchequer, with the Labour Party not only "In" but also OUT of what to me always appeared to be its obscurantium. I mean, with the public ownership of the Bank put first on its program. A great deal of what you probably considered my moonshine (if you ever considered it at all) must now be made open to the British public.

All over the place what were 20 years ago considered heresies of my friends are now admitted as fact. The "A" plus "B" theory of Maj. C. H. Douglas is tacitly accepted in all proposals for government spending. The public has learned a great deal, but it still has the right to know MORE. If that be over my dead body so much the worse both for me and for the public.

BUT the suppression of historic fact has NOT been useful, it neither helped to preserve peace nor to carry on the war. Given the present tension, no one is more ready than I to admit that certain facts should perhaps not be dragged into the limelight at this moment.

BUT that does not apply to other facts that are simply ignored. I mean that the men in charge both of England and the U. S. A. seem still unaware of them. And that after 25 years of study I can no longer be treated as a whimsical child in these matters.

I am sorry to take up so much space, but I cannot tell from your letter whether you have had enough information to see clearly.

The agent of the Dept. of Justice started by saying that they proposed to consider my past 30 years work. I do not know whether Mr. Stryker would be prepared for such labour, and without it, I do not know how he could tell the Court what the case is about.

The picture painted by propaganda has been such, that I do not know whether you can conceive that FREE SPEECH was preserved precisely where the British Public would least expect it, namely in Italy by a few unknown, I suppose you would call them "liberals" working inside the Italian frame work. I do not think it is an occasion for great skill in presenting a case so much as for great patience in making clear the bearing of known and knowable facts. Which facts, I am not sure whether you yet grasp, if you will pardon a rather flat statement.

What I am in absolute ignorance of is: whether anyone actually heard my broadcasts; whether they did any good, by which I mean whether they in any way contributed to the better understanding of certain economic fundamentals. Which better understanding is definitely shown now in public pronouncements in England and the U. S. A. (As C. H. Douglas used to say after the other war: "If they dont do it now, they will have to do it after the next one".)

I do not know whether the public HEARD, or if hearing they understood one single word of my talks. The only auditors I know of were foreigners in Florence. Plus whatever education one could insert in Berlin. Yes, the RE-education of Europe. Any enlightenment on that point that you can give me, I would be most grateful to receive. And, of course, seeing that "my program" is going through all over the place. I can not know that those who are putting it through are in any way conscious of my existence, or that they would be pleased to know that I had been on their side of the battle for enlightenment.

Don't gasp I know it will take time for this strange view to get through the probable mist of prejudice that has been raised by the jingo press.

But a great deal that could in 1938 only be printed in outcast periodicals of small circulation, is now in print and will increasingly be printed in the more general press.

I want very much to know the source or reason for your opinion that I should not address the Court. Is it due to your not knowing what I actually said on the air?

I will send you a copy of this letter in 2 days time and if you receive both copies you can send one to Mr. MacLeish. If you receive only one copy, would you please have it copied and send him a copy?

It seems to me he might also communicate with Roger Baldwin of the Civil Liberties Union as the question of Freedom of speech on the air, together with other constitutional points should interest them.

Emphatically I want to see Mr. MacLeish and have been given to understand that it would be possible once I were in the U. S. A.

BUT the simplest plan would be for him to write to me as my lawyer (if I am correct in supposing that he is a lawyer) at any rate he has known my work for 20 years and has some concept of what I have been driving at . . . am not in the least sure that Ll. Stryker has, or could have.

Can Omar do anything towards getting his mother's passport put in order. There seems to be some circumlocution re the formalities.

Have I a balance at Faber and Fabers that could be sent to Dorothy pending the release of her own funds?

Also can you ask Mr. Eliot whether Faber will be ready to print another volume of Cantos? or at any rate "The Testament of Confucius". This is a new translation of the Ta S'eu; and the first proper translation of the Chung Yung, plus an abridgement of the analects and of Mencius.

He may understand from the Cantos on the Chinese Dynasties, that this text of Confucius, having been at the root of the DOUBLE chinese dynasties is the ONLY basis on which a world order can work.

The Chinese Empire during its great periods offering the ONLY working model (and having served repeatedly as proof of being a working model) that can possibly serve in the present situation.

This may sound a large order, but we have come through a very large war. And someone has got to use adult intelligence in dealing with the world problem.

Confucius started as market inspector, and rose to be Prime Minister AND resigned. He gave more thought to the problem of vast administration than any simple high-brow philosopher.

I do not know that I would have arrived at the centre of his meaning if I had not been down under the collapse of a regime. But at any rate the work is serious. I mean the translation. Both the First and Second book have been published here, I mean my Italian translation of the Ta S'eu with the Chinese text facing it and my Italian version of the Chung Yung. I was working on the Mencius when the partigiani came to the front door with a tommy-gun.

Another point that you may not know, i.e. that I was not fleeing from justice. You may still be under innumerable misapprehensions.

I dont want to extend the present letter indefinitely.

Sincerely yours,

EZRA POUND

III

ARRAIGNMENT

ON NOVEMBER 7, 1945 I read in the morning newspaper that Pound would soon be brought to the United States for trial. The same day I wrote to Attorney General Tom C. Clark advising him that I had been retained to confer with Pound about his defense and asking to be informed when he arrived. A few days later I received a telegram from the Attorney General's office that Pound had been brought to Washington and was in the District of Columbia jail. Here is the newspaper account of his expected arrival as announced by the Attorney General.

NEW YORK TIMES, NOVEMBER 7, 1945

WASHINGTON, Nov. 6, 1945.—Ezra Pound, the American writer who broadcast Axis propaganda from Rome during the war, will be brought to Washington next week preparatory to his trial for treason.

Attorney General Tom Clark stated at a news conference that six Italians would arrive here tonight or tomorrow as witnesses against Pound. The Department of Justice will question these persons so that they will be ready to give testimony before a grand jury of the District of Columbia.

The jury, however, cannot start its work until Pound is actually here. He will arrive by airplane in the custody of Army officers.

To establish treason, two witnesses must have seen the act. Mr. Clark said the persons arriving here were in the radio studio when Pound made his broadcasts, and thus could swear to the circumstance. The Department of Justice has also collected phonograph records and original scripts from which Pound worked in Rome and will present these as part of the evidence. * * *

The following day I had a talk with the Chief of the Criminal Division of the Department of Justice, Mr. McInerney, and with his assistant who would have charge of the prosecution, Isaiah Matlack. They arranged for me to see Pound at the District of Columbia jail. I also had a talk with the superintendent of the jail and with the Chief Judge of the District of Columbia District Court, Bolitha J. Laws.

Judge Laws said that he was very happy to know that I was going to appear for Pound because a Washington criminal lawyer of somewhat dubious reputation had been boasting that he was going to get Pound's case. I entered an appearance before Judge Laws after arranging for a Washington attorney of my acquaintance to introduce me formally to the court, as is the custom when a lawyer appears in a jurisdiction where he is not a member of the bar. All this was reported the next day to Laughlin and Moore in the following letter:

LETTER FROM JULIEN CORNELL TO JAMES LAUGHLIN

November 21, 1945

Dear J.:

After making arrangements to get in to see him, I went down to Washington Monday evening and spent two hours with Pound yesterday morning.

I found the poor devil in a rather desperate condition. He is very wobbly in his mind and while his talk is entirely rational, he flits from one idea to another and is unable to concentrate even to the extent of answering a single question without immediately wandering off the subject. We spent most of the time talking about Confucius, Jefferson and the economic and political implications of their ideas. I let him ramble on, even though I did not get much of the information which I wanted, as it seemed a shame to deprive him of the pleasure of talking, which has been almost entirely denied to him for a long while.

Although I am not sure of the precise facts, I gather that he had been placed in solitary confinement immediately after his arrest and held incommunicado, being told that nobody knew where he was, or what happened to him. He was put in an open cage so that the guards could watch him for possible suicide attempts, and during the day he sat in the broiling sun on the plains at Pisa, while at night searchlights beat down upon him. He was unable to talk to anyone and had no reading material except two volumes of Confucius which he has been translating from the Chinese. As a result, he went out of his mind and suffered complete loss of memory, a state from which he said he did not fully recover until September, and I would say that he is still under a considerable mental cloud. For instance, he kept talking about the possibility that powerful government officials with whom he had no acquaintance whatever might interest themselves in his case if they could be persuaded of the soundness of his economic views. He said that whether or not he is convicted he could be of tremendous help to President Truman, because of his knowledge of conditions in Italy and Japan. He added, with a wry smile, that the greatest benefit which can come to a poet is to be hung.

I am planning to make an application for bail, which the government will probably oppose, but not strenuously, since they regard Pound's case as rather a mild one of its kind. I intend to support the application by showing that his health has been seriously impaired by the brutal nature of his confinement and that his continued imprisonment may end both his life and his sanity. Even three army psychiatrists who examined him found that he was suffering from claustrophobia.

I discussed with him the possibility of pleading insanity as a defense and he has no objection. In fact he told me that the idea had already occurred to him. In view of what we now know of his recent medical history, I think there is a good chance that such a defense might succeed. As you probably know, the trial of such an issue is almost always a farce, since learned medicos who testify for each side squarely contradict each other and completely befuddle the jury. It then largely becomes a question of the sympathy of the jury, assuming, of course, that there is no question of outright faking.

I have entered an appearance as counsel for Mr. Pound with the permission of the Chief Justice of the District Court for the District of Columbia with whom I discussed the case briefly yesterday and found him most courteous and helpful. I told the court, however, that my appearance was for the purpose of arraignment, which includes entering of a plea to the indictment and application for bail, and that I am not prepared to say at the present time whether I am in a position to take the defense. This depends somewhat upon the course which the defense will take, and it may be necessary to retain some other trial counsel, although I am quite willing to represent him for the purpose of arranging the defense and advising him clear through.

I told him that I want to postpone a decision as to who should represent him on the trial until I know more about the case, and he appeared to agree to all these suggestions.

I am sending a copy of this letter to Mr. Moore. For his benefit, I should like to say that in this country the functions of solicitor and barrister are combined, one or more members of a firm specializing in trial work, but never to the exclusion of office practice, and in many cases both functions are combined in one person, as in my case.

With best regards,

Sincerely yours,

JULIEN

P. S. Pound wants you to publish his translations of Confucius, which are ready, and also a new volume of Cantos, some of which I believe he sent out from prison in Italy. He seems to think the Confucius is world shaking in its import and should be published immediately.

It was apparent to me when I first interviewed Pound that he was in no state to stand trial or even plead to the indictment but was in need of medical care and hospital treatment. Therefore, I advised him to stand mute when the indictment was read to him and that I would inform the court that he was in no condition to plead. I told Pound that I would then make a motion asking the court to admit him to bail so that he could be sent to a hospital. In support of the motion, I prepared an affidavit disclosing Pound's condition and a brief, showing that there were precedents for his being admitted to bail despite the fact that treason is a capital offense. The brief is given in an appendix. Here is the text of my affidavit:

AFFIDAVIT OF JULIEN CORNELL FILED IN UNITED STATES DISTRICT COURT FOR THE DISTRICT OF COLUMBIA, NOVEMBER 27, 1945, IN SUPPORT OF APPLICATION FOR BAIL

JULIEN CORNELL, being duly sworn deposes and says:

I am an attorney at law of New York and have appeared herein for the defendant, EZRA POUND, at the request of his London solicitors, and with the permission of the court, for the sole purpose of his arraignment.

I must report that the defendant, Ezra Pound, after his arrest on a charge of treason last May, has been continuously held incommunicado in solitary confinement, under such extreme conditions that he suffered a complete mental collapse and loss of memory. Although he has partially recovered his health, I believe that he is still insane and that if he remains in prison he may never recover, and not only will he be unable to stand trial on this indictment, but one of the greatest literary geniuses of these times will be permanently eclipsed. I urge this court to order his removal at once from the District of Columbia jail, where he is now confined, to a civilian mental hospital or sanatorium under bail, or that if bail is not permitted, he be removed to a civilian mental hospital or sanatorium operated by the United States and placed in custody of a civilian physician. I believe that such action is imperative, and that if it is not taken immediately, he will never recover his senses sufficiently to defend himself against the indictment which has been handed up to the court.

This affidavit is accompanied by a memorandum of law relating to the crime charged, showing that the statutes permit the admission of the defendant to bail, although treason is a capital offense. This affidavit will be confined to the facts in the case, which are stated to the best of my information and belief, to the extent necessary for the purposes of the relief now prayed for. In order to furnish the court with further information about the defendant, if desired, I have appended as Exhibit A, a copy of the only material concerning him which has been published currently, namely, an article which appeared in the newspaper "PM" (New York) for November 25, 1945.

Since the release of the defendant from prison depends upon the likelihood that he will not attempt to leave the jurisdiction of the court while the trial is pending, I shall acquaint the court briefly with his history before proceeding to the particulars bearing directly upon the present application.

Ezra Pound is now sixty years of age. He was born at Hailey, Idaho, on October 30, 1885 of Quaker and New England stock, his forebears, which include members of the Loomis, Wadsworth and Weston families, having emigrated to this country from England with the early colonists. His grandfather, Thaddeus C. Pound, was a member of Congress from Wisconsin in 1878 and also was Acting Governor of that state. His father during most of his life served the United States Treasury in a technical capacity at the Philadelphia mint.

Pound was educated at Hamilton College, Clinton, New York, from which he was graduated in 1905 with the degree of Ph. B. and the University of Pennsylvania where he received an M. A. degree. He was also awarded the honorary degree of D. Litt. by Hamilton College in 1939, and cited by the college in these terms, which give some indication of his tremendous stature in the field of letters:

> EZRA POUND:—Native of Idaho, graduate of Hamilton College in the Class of 1905, poet, critic, and prose writer of great distinction. Since completing your college career you have had a life full of significance in the arts. You have found that you could work more happily in Europe than in America and so have lived most of the past thirty years an expatriate making your home in England, France, and Italy, but your writings are known wherever English is read. Your feet have trodden paths, however, where the great read-

> ing public could give you few followers—into provençal and Italian poetry, into Anglo-Saxon and Chinese. From all of these excursions you have brought back treasure. Your translations from the Chinese have, for example, led one of the most gifted of contemporary poets to call you the inventor of Chinese poetry of our time. Your Alma Mater, however, is an old lady who has not always understood where you were going, but she has watched you with interest and pride if not always with understanding. The larger public has also been at times amazed at your political and economic as well as your artistic credo, and you have retaliated by making yourself—not unintentionally perhaps—their gadfly. Your range of interests is immense, and whether or not your theories of society survive, your name is permanently linked with the development of English poetry in the twentieth century. Your reputation is international, you have guided many poets into new paths, you have pointed new directions, and the historian of the future in tracing the development of your growing mind will inevitably, we are happy to think, be led to Hamilton and to the influence of your college teachers. You have ever been a generous champion of younger writers as well as artists in other fields, and for this fine and rare human quality and for your own achievements in poetry and prose, we honor you.

The trail which brought Pound into such distinction at the hands of his countrymen led entirely along foreign paths, beginning soon after he left college when he made his abode in Venice. In 1908 he published there his first volume of verse, *A Lume Spento.* The following year saw publication in London of more verses under the titles *Personae* and *Exultations.*

The vast spread of Pound's abilities began to appear in this early period, when he became known as an art critic, and as the champion of new schools of literature and music, as well as for his poetry. He was among the first to recognize the writer James Joyce, the poet Rabindranath Tagore, the sculptor Gaudier Brzeska and the composer Antheil.

The influence on poetry of the Imagist school was due largely to Pound's support, which included his collection of Imagist poems published in 1914.

His roving mind turned at this time to the Orient, as he translated and published Chinese and Japanese poetry and drama, thereby arousing public interest in the literature of the East.

In 1920 Pound left England to make his home in Paris, where he continued to write for British magazines, translated French poetry, and even composed the musical score for an opera, *Villon,* which was sung in Paris. Not the least of his works is his *ABC of Economics,* an amazingly clear exposition of his novel economic theories.

In the decade following the First World War, Pound had published most of his forty volumes of verse, criticism, history, and economic theory. He had known in his ascendancy such fame and recognition as rarely comes to a writer even after his death. This is the more remarkable because Pound was always a pioneer, exploring new and untrodden ways.

In the full bloom of his mature period he left Paris for the solitude and quiet of the Italian Riviera, settling in 1924 at Rapallo, where he lived until the outbreak of the late war. Here he began work on his monumental *Cantos,* while continuing his many interests and activities.

In 1939, when it appeared that war was approaching and that the United States might be involved, Pound journeyed back to his native land, where he saw such statesmen as Bankhead, Borah, Bridges, Byrd, Downey, Lodge, MacLeish, Tinkham, Voorhis and Wallace, all in a vain effort to move the nation's policies toward paths which he thought were the paths to peace. Failing in this task, he returned to Rapallo where he lived with his family until the Germans drove them back into the hills.

Early in May of this year, Pound accosted the first American he saw, a Negro soldier advancing with the native *partigiani,* by whom he was taken at his own request to an American command post at Lavagna, whence he was sent to the army's Counter Information Center at Genoa. Pound was under house arrest during this time, being treated as a political prisoner.

After several weeks at Genoa, Pound was handcuffed and taken away by military police in a jeep, naively believing that he was bound for an airport and a plane to the United States. But his actual destination was an American military prison at Pisa.

He was at once beset with fears—that he would be thrown with murderers and felons who would kill him; that nobody knew where he was and nobody would ever know what happened to him.

Pound was placed in solitary confinement in a steel cage specially built for him in the prison yard. He knew not whether he would rot away in this cage or be taken out and hanged as a traitor. But far worse than these was the thought that his wife and daughter would never know his fate, and would dream, until they reached their own graves, of the agony interred in his. Not far away were the pens in which long term offenders were confined, but all other prisoners were forbidden to speak to Pound, and could not come near him. Not only was the prisoner deprived of all human companionship, but he was given no reading matter to relax his fevered brain. He had nothing to employ his time but a Chinese text of Confucius which he had been translating, nothing to distract his mind from worry and fear.

And such mental torture was not all he suffered. It was now full summer, and the Italian sun beat down on the prison yard with unbearable intensity. A military highway ran nearby, and having no shelter, he could not escape the ceaseless noise and dust. Although all the other prisoners were supplied with tents to keep out the heat and glare of the sun, Pound was given no such protection, probably so that guards could watch him at all times. Whereas other prisoners were let out of the cages for meals and exercise, Pound was always confined. While others were penned up in groups, he was alone in his cage.

After enduring the tropical sun all day, neither sleep nor rest came with the night—electric lights glared into the poet's cage and burned into his bloodshot eyes. The cage was devoid of all furniture. Pound lay upon the cement floor in his blankets, broiled by the sun and wet by the rain.

After about three weeks of struggle to maintain his sanity, the wretched man fell ill. The heat and the glare, added to the hopelessness of being held incommunicado and the torture of solitary confinement, were more than his aging mind could bear. Pound was stricken with violent and hysterical terror. He lost his memory. He became desperately thin and weak until finally the prison doctor feared for him.

Pound was then taken out of his unhappy cage and placed in a tent. He was given a cot to lie upon, and medical treatment. The doctor even prescribed a walk each day, but most often the guards neglected to take him out for exercise.

While the doctors took measures to keep Pound's body alive, his mind was not rescued. He was still kept in solitary confinement, still held incommunicado, still deprived of all reading matter but religious tracts. As physical strength gradually flowed back into his body, the terror and hysteria subsided somewhat, memory returned, but the great mind remained impaired, and fits of shuddering terror balked his struggle to regain his senses.

Not until October 3rd could the prisoner communicate with the outside world. On that day his wife was allowed to see him for half an hour. Two weeks later he saw his daughter for a like period, and on November 3rd his wife was again permitted to visit him. These visits helped to restore him to some outward semblance of his former self.

A week or so ago, Pound being strong enough to travel, he was taken by jeep to Rome and thence by plane to Washington, where he arrived on November 18th, and has since remained, in the District of Columbia jail.

I respectfully pray that the defendant be admitted to bail on the ground that he may be safely released without fear that he would attempt to flee the jurisdiction, and on the further ground that his release under bail is necessary in order that he may secure proper medical treatment. If the court determines that the defendant should not be admitted to bail, I urge that he be removed at once from imprisonment in a penal institution and that he be placed in the custody of one or more physicians in a civilian hospital or sanatorium operated by the United States or by the District of Columbia. Only in a normal environment, free from the drastic restraints which are necessary in penal hospitals, can he possibly recover, in my opinion;

only by such medical treatment does he stand a chance of regaining his sanity even to the point where he could stand trial on this indictment.

I am confident that a disinterested psychiatric investigation of his condition would show that such measures are imperative.

JULIEN CORNELL

The indictment handed up to the court by a grand jury at the October 1945 term charged that Pound, an American citizen owing allegiance to the United States, had committed the crime of treason by adhering to the enemies of the United States, the Kingdom of Italy and its military allies, and giving them aid and comfort by accepting employment as a radio propagandist from the Italian government and making speeches over the Rome radio on a number of dates mentioned in the indictment. The indictment also charged that Pound received remuneration from the Italian government in the amount of 750 lire, a paltry sum which he claimed did not cover his expense of going down to Rome to make a broadcast. The text of the indictment is given in an appendix; also the text of my brief in regard to bail.

The courtroom was crowded when Pound appeared before Judge Laws to plead to the indictment. He said not a word but sat with hands folded and eyes downcast while I told the court that he was not in condition to make a plea and asked Judge Laws to enter a plea of not guilty for him. I then handed up to Judge Laws my motion papers, at the same time giving copies to Isaiah Matlack, Assistant Attorney General in charge of the prosecution. I explained orally the general tenor of my motion, which was that Pound was suffering from mental illness, that he was physically fatigued and at the point of exhaustion from the rigors of his confinement at the concentration camp (there is no other word for it) of the United States Army at Pisa, that he was in urgent need of medical care, and that in my opinion he never should have been sent over here for trial. In view of the urgency of the situation, I asked the Judge to order Pound's immediate removal from jail to a hospital.

Matlack expressed himself as completely taken by surprise at this disclosure. He asked for time to read the motion papers and consult with his superiors. After a brief recess, Matlack said that the government had no objection to a medical examination and the judge ordered Pound transferred to Gallinger Hospital, a general hospital in the District of Columbia.

On the following pages are Judge Laws' decision referring Pound to the hospital, a newspaper account of the arraignment, and a letter which I wrote to Mr. Moore explaining what had happened.

DECISION OF CHIEF JUSTICE BOLITHA J. LAWS, NOVEMBER 27, 1945

I have considered the motion filed in behalf of the defendant that he be admitted to bail or in the alternative that he be removed from his present place of imprisonment in the Washington Asylum and Jail to the custody of a hospital or other institution operated by the United States or the District of Columbia. From the showing made before me by counsel for the defendant, it appears advisable to have an examination and observation of the defendant made by physicians and that pending such an examination and report of their findings and pending the granting of opportunity to counsel for the prosecution to reply to the motion for bail, no action should be taken on such motion.

Accordingly, the defendant is ordered remanded to the Washington Asylum and Jail with the recommendation that he be transferred to Gallinger Hospital or such other hospital as may be designated by authorized officials of the United States for examination and observation and for treatment, if found necessary. The motion for admission to bail is continued for further hearing until December 14, 1945; counsel for the United States will submit on or before December 10th any showing which they may desire to make in opposition to the said motion.

BOLITHA J. LAWS,
Chief Justice

NEW YORK HERALD TRIBUNE, NOVEMBER 28, 1945

WASHINGTON, Nov. 27, 1945—Unkempt and clad in G. I. hand-me-downs, Ezra Pound, sixty-year-old American poet accused of treason, stood mute today during arraignment before a Federal district court here, shuffling from one foot to the other while a defense attorney requested that he be released from the District of Columbia jail because he suffers claustrophobia and may lose his sanity if he remains imprisoned.

Chief Justice Bolitha Laws remanded Pound to Gallinger Hospital for examination.

The defense attorney, Julien Cornell, of New York, said Pound lacked sufficient judgment at present to make any plea before the court, and asked Justice Laws to enter a plea of "not guilty" for him.

Mr. Cornell told the court that Pound was unable to enter a plea as the result of * * * claustrophobia ever since imprisonment by the Army at Pisa, Italy, where he was held seven months "incommunicado" in a cage made of air landing strips welded together.

Mr. Cornell said the stay at the District of Columbia jail had "become unbearable" for the poet after a jail break caused authorities to keep all prisoners in their cells without customary exercise walks. * * *

Pound was imprisoned early in May this year and was not removed from Pisa until Saturday, when he was flown to Washington for arraignment and trial.

Prosecuting attorneys had expected the defendant to request an early trial. "It's a complete surprise," Isaiah Matlack, justice department counsel in charge of the government case, declared. * * *

Pound, by today's court order, will be held at Gallinger Hospital for examination and observation and treatment if necessary until December 14.

He was re-indicted yesterday by a Federal Grand Jury for "nineteen overt acts of treason" between December 11, 1941, and May 3, 1945, including charges that he gave aid and comfort to the enemy by accepting employment for the Italian fascist government as a radio propagandist and for counseling enemy officials in operations against the United States. He was originally indicted in July, 1943.

LETTER FROM JULIEN CORNELL TO ARTHUR V. MOORE

November 29, 1945

Dear Mr. Moore:

Ezra Pound has been reindicted on substantially the same grounds and appeared for arraignment in the United States District Court for the District of Columbia on November 27th before the Chief Justice, Bolitha J. Laws. I informed the court that Mr. Pound had reached a state of physical and mental exhaustion, due to the hardships of his journey to this country and subsequent confinement, which made it impossible for him to plead to the indictment.

While he is able to converse extensively about literary and political matters, he appears to have great difficulty in concentrating upon his case and he appears to be unable to exercise any judgment whatever regarding the impending trial. Because of his lack of ability to exercise any judgment and also because of his mental exhaustion, I considered him unable to plead to the indictment and requested the court that he be permitted to stand mute. Under our laws, when a defendant stands mute, a plea of not guilty must be entered by the court, and this was done.

I then went on to explain to the court the history of Mr. Pound's incarceration at Pisa and the insanity which resulted therefrom. I told the court that in my opinion Mr. Pound was on the verge of a second mental collapse, and that his sanity, if not his life, required that he be immediately removed from the prison and placed in a hospital for observation and treatment.

The attorneys for the government expressed themselves as taken by surprise at this disclosure, although they had ample opportunity to discover the facts. They made no objection, however, to Mr. Pound's removal from prison and the judge thereupon entered an order directing that he be transferred to Gallinger Hospital, Washington, D. C. where he will receive a psychiatric examination and his medical needs will be attended to. I am planning to have an outstanding psychiatrist make an examination for the defense and his report together with the report of the government's physicians will be presented to the court in a few weeks' time. After Mr. Pound's mental and physical condition has been investigated by the physicians, there will be a further hearing upon my motion that he be admitted to bail, consideration of which the court has postponed pending the medical investigation.

If some such arrangement is not made, he will not be able to get the treatment which I feel sure he needs, namely, relaxation, recreation and a certain amount of physical freedom. Unless he is admitted to bail or paroled in the custody of a physician or hospital official, he will have to remain either in prison or in a hospital where he would be confined to his room because there happens to be no government hospital in the District of Columbia which affords adequate facilities for an ambulatory patient.

I think there is serious doubt whether Mr. Pound will be able to recover sufficient strength to go through the long ordeal of the trial, unless he is allowed to go to a sanatorium or convalescent hospital such as I shall urge upon the court. I think it quite probable, therefore, that the government will eventually have to take the proper measures to restore him to physical and mental health, as otherwise they will never be able to try him, since I feel quite sure that he would break down before the trial could be completed. However, the report of the doctors will probably shed additional light on his condition.

Even without medical opinion, however, you can judge from reading the affidavit describing his breakdown at Pisa (which I am sending you by ocean mail since it is rather bulky), that he is very near the end of his resources. I am also sending you by ocean mail a memorandum of law on the matter of bail which I submitted to the court, and which may be of some interest to you and will inform you of the nature of the proceedings taken thus far.

If bail is allowed, I have some hope that it may be possible to raise sufficient security in this country so that it will not be necessary to have Mrs. Pound's funds put up as security. I have made inquiries of American bonding companies, and find that none of them are so situated that they could write a bail bond secured by British funds, although it may be that you could find some way to do this through Lloyds.

You will be pleased to know that Mr. Pound's friends in the United States are deeply concerned over his welfare and anxious to help him. Among those whom I know to be concerned, in addition to Mr. MacLeish, are Ernest Hemingway, H. L. Mencken and E. E. Cummings. In addition, he has two very old and good friends living in Washington, Ida and Adah Lee Mapel, who have known him for 40 years, and they have been to see him and will continue to visit him regularly. I am sure they will give him much comfort.

You will be interested to know that I succeeded in obtaining the release from the authorities of Mr. Pound's manuscripts, including the additional Cantos and the translations from Confucius. He wants both of these published and suggested that publication on your side might be undertaken by Faber and Faber.

Sincerely yours,

JULIEN CORNELL

IV

MEDICAL EXAMINATION

THE NEXT STEP was to arrange for a psychiatrist to examine my client. A lawyer of my acquaintance told me that the best psychiatrist in Washington was Dr. Winfred Overholser. I sent him a telegram inquiring whether his services would be available but learned that he could not undertake it because he was a government official, being in charge of St. Elizabeths Hospital in Washington and unable tc take a private case. My next thought was the famous Dr. Adolf Meyer of Baltimore. Dr. Meyer declined on the ground that he was an invalid and could not leave his home but he recommended several other doctors, including Dr. Wendell Muncie, connected with Johns Hopkins University. Dr. Muncie agreed to take the case.

I was reasonably certain that Pound would never go to trial. It was obvious to me even at my first interview with him that he had very little understanding of the fix which he was in and that he would be incapable of preparing a defense or participating in a trial. He simply could not comprehend the realities of his situation. I was reasonably sure that any impartial psychiatrist would reach the conclusion that Pound should not be tried, but what usually happens in such cases is that the doctor for the prosecution testifies that the man is sufficiently sane to be tried while the doctor for the defense testifies to the contrary and the jury must choose between them. This was the first treason case to reach the courts. It had aroused much excitement in some quarters and it was hard to tell, in an electrically charged atmosphere, what a jury might do.

But Pound's trial was not my immediate concern. The man was too ill for that. He was in dire need of medical care. Therefore in arranging for Dr. Muncie to examine him, the thought which was uppermost in my mind was to convince Judge Laws that Pound should be released on bail so that he could be placed in a hospital and receive proper care. Although bail is very unusual in capital cases, the statutes permit it even in the case of treason, and under the circumstances I was hopeful that Pound could be released to a hospital. The situation was outlined in a letter which I wrote to Dr. Muncie as follows:

LETTER FROM JULIEN CORNELL TO DR. WENDELL MUNCIE

December 6, 1945

Dear Dr. Muncie:

This will confirm the arrangement made by exchange of telegrams under which you have agreed to make a psychiatric examination of Ezra Pound on Thursday or Friday of next week at Gallinger Hospital in order to determine whether, in your opinion, he is sufficiently sane to stand trial for treason in the United States District Court for the District of Columbia. A written report of your findings should be prepared for submission to the court, and if the court desires it, it may be necessary for you to appear in person, although I believe for present purposes a written statement will suffice.

It is possible that the court will order a jury trial of the issue of sanity, in which case I should want you to testify in behalf of the defendant. The present examination, however, is merely for the purpose of aiding the court in determining whether to admit the defendant to bail or remand him to prison, and also to determine whether *prima facie* evidence of insanity exists so that a trial of that issue should be ordered.

In order to assist you in making the examination, I should like to give you something of Mr. Pound's history. You are probably familiar in a general way with his literary achievements. There is enclosed a copy of an article which appeared in the newspaper PM November 25, 1945 which will give you some idea of his life and works.

I enclose a copy of the only complete transcript of a broadcast which has come into my possession. This was delivered over the Rome radio on April 23, 1942. Pound says that all the broadcasts were his own ideas alone and no one ever told him what to say. In fact it was announced over the radio that Pound was not being asked to say anything contrary to his conscience or his duties as an American citizen. Furthermore, he was paid for making the broadcasts only about $17 each, which was hardly sufficient to cover his transportation from Rapallo to Rome. I believe that the government has investigated this phase of the broadcasts, and Pound's story in this respect could be corroborated by the government's own investigations.

Apart from any question of whether Pound's mind was affected at the time when he was making the broadcasts and in prior years, it is conceded by the government that he became definitely insane during his imprisonment in Italy last summer. When the American forces reached the north of Italy, Pound surrendered himself and was taken to the Counter Information Center of the army at Genoa in May 1945. Here he was held under house arrest as a political prisoner for several weeks. He was interviewed by a representative of the Department of Justice who came up from Rome, of whom he requested that he be permitted to return to the United States. Pound states that he had no idea that he would be indicted for treason, but he wanted to come back to this country in order to give to President Truman the benefit of his intimate knowledge of conditions in Italy and Japan. He was somewhat surprised therefore, when instead of being put on board a plane for the United States, he was taken to a military prison at Pisa. This was at the end of May or the beginning of June, 1945.

Not only was Pound deprived of rest by reason of the intense heat and glare, but he had no recreation or relaxation whatever. He was not allowed to leave his cage for meals and exercise like the other prisoners, but was at all times kept in solitary confinement. None of the other prisoners were permitted to speak to him. He had no reading matter except two volumes of the Chinese text of Confucius which he had been translating into English.

After a week or so of the mental and physical torment of confinement in the cage, Pound's mind gave way. He says that he can now recall only the sensation that the top of his head was empty;

also that his eyebrows were constantly taut in a raised position, due to the heat and glare. As a result of the hardships of his imprisonment he was stricken with violent terror and hysteria, and also affected with amnesia. As a result of Pound's condition he was removed from the cage and placed in the shelter of a tent. He was also given a cot to lie upon and medical treatment. Gradually he recovered his health, but his mind apparently remained affected, perhaps due to the fact that he was still held incommunicado and in solitary confinement, and he was still given no recreation or relaxation, being confined to the reading of religious tracts. He says that one thing which helped to save his sanity during this period was the discovery of an anthology of poetry in the privy; also the kindness shown to him by a colored soldier who brought him his meals. The latter was the only person who was able to speak to him, and although he was confined to remarks about the food, he managed to convey sufficient sympathy by voice and glance as to give much comfort to his fellow prisoner.

I have read through the poetry which Pound wrote while he was in prison and extracted the only lines which show a reaction to his imprisonment and which might afford some evidence of his mental condition at that time. A copy of these verses is enclosed.

It was not until October 3rd that Pound was permitted to communicate with the outside world. On that day he saw his wife for half an hour. Two weeks later he saw his daughter for a like period, and on November 3rd his wife was again allowed to visit him.

Early in November Pound was deemed strong enough to make the trip back to the United States and was taken by jeep to Rome and thence by plane to Washington. When he arrived in Washington he was near physical exhaustion, having been kept up all night in the jeep and again lacking sleep in the plane. He arrived Sunday night, November 18th, and the next day was taken to court. I saw him for the first time on Tuesday, November 20th. He appeared then very tired but most happy to see some one sent by his friends. I found it impossible to discuss his case with him, as it seemed to distress him and he avoided answering the few questions which I directed at him along that line. He talked freely about himself and his literary interests.

The poor physical condition in which I found him was aggravated by the fact that on Friday, November 23rd, he was taken in the police van to the "bull pen" at the courthouse and kept there all day shut in with a group of prisoners, presumably because the Grand Jury was that day in the process of indicting him. And again on November 24th and 25th he was subjected to further suffering by reason of being locked in his cell together with all other prisoners at the District jail, as a result of a jail break. This was a great hardship on him because he suffers from claustrophobia. Being locked up for two days drove him almost to the point of mental collapse. He thereupon requested to be taken to the infirmary at the jail where he spent Sunday night, November 25th. When I saw him on Tuesday morning, November 27th, he was in a state of almost complete mental and physical exhaustion. I spent about one hour with him reading over some of his poems, and at the end of the hour I mentioned for the first time the proceedings in court scheduled for that afternoon. I told him that he was to be arraigned and that he would have to plead to the indictment. I suggested that because of his condition it might be wise for him to remain mute rather than enter a plea of not guilty, and explained to him the implications of each course of proceeding. When I asked him whether he wanted to stand mute or would prefer to enter a plea, he was unable to answer me. His mouth opened once or twice as if to speak, but no words came out. He looked up at the ceiling and his face began to twitch. Finally he said he felt ill and asked if he could not go back to the infirmary.

I got this same reaction, although less pronounced, on previous occasions when I sought to question him upon matters bearing on his case.

Accordingly when Pound was arraigned that afternoon I told the court that he was not sufficiently well to enter a plea and he was permitted to remain mute and seated. Under such circumstances the court was obliged by law to enter a plea of not guilty.

In examining Mr. Pound I wish you would bear in mind that there is another question involved in addition to his sanity, namely, the question whether even if he is sane, he is sufficiently well to stand the ordeal of a lengthy trial. This would require several weeks of conferences with his attorneys in preparation for trial, and probably two weeks at least of proceedings in court. I have some reason to fear that even if he were sufficiently sane to understand the proceedings, the ordeal of the trial might bring on a relapse.

Sincerely yours,

JULIEN CORNELL

LINES FROM THE PISAN CANTOS OF EZRA POUND ENCLOSED WITH FOREGOING LETTER

That from the gates of death,
    that from the gates of death : Whitman or Lovelace
        found on the jo-house seat at that
in a cheap edition,*
            when the raft broke and the waters went over me,
hast thou swum in a sea of air strip
    thru an aeon of nothingness,
Immacolata, Introibo
    for those who drink of the bitterness
Perpetua, Agatha, Anastasia
            saeculorum
repos donnez a cils
    senza termine funge Immaculata Regina
        Les larmes que j'ai crées m'inondent
Tard, tres tard je t'ai connu, la Tristesse
I have been hard as youth sixty years
        if calm be after tempest

---

* This refers to the anthology of poetry which Pound found in the privy.

that the ants seem to wobble
as the morning sun catches their shadows
(Nadasky, Duett, McAlister),†
also Comfort K. P. special mention
on sick call Penrieth, Turner, Toth hieri
(no fortune and with a name to come)
Bankers, Seitz, Hildebrand and Corneilson
Armstrong Special mention K. P.†
Wiseman (not William) africanus.
with a smoky torch thru the unending
labyrinth of the souterrain
or remembering Carleton let him celebrate Christ in the
grain
and if the corn cat be beaten
Demeter has lain in my furrow
This wind is lighter than swansdown
the day moves not at all
(Zupp, Bufford and Bohon)†
men of no fortune and with a name to come
his helmet is used for a pisspot
this helmet is used for my footbath
Elpenor can count the shingle under Zoagli,
Pepitone†† was wasting toothwash
as I lay by the drain hole
the guard's opinion is lower than that of the prisoner's

At this time, I inquired of a number of Pound's literary friends whether they had any knowledge of Pound or correspondence with him which would shed light upon his condition. Among others, I approached T. S. Eliot, Ernest Hemingway, E. E. Cummings, Archibald MacLeish and Allen Tate. From these and other friends of

† The names of prisoners as called out by a guard.
†† A guard.

Pound, this picture emerged: a brilliant literary genius who lived in a rarefied atmosphere of his own creation, kind and generous toward his friends, vituperative and scurrilous toward his fancied enemies, including public figures whom he did not even know, a man of enormous ego. Some thought that he was merely eccentric; others that his mental aberration bordered on the abnormal.

Ernest Hemingway wrote me a most interesting letter in December, 1945 which I passed along to Dr. Muncie. Unfortunately this letter cannot be printed here because Hemingway in his will directed that none of his letters should ever be published. Hemingway expressed a great admiration for Pound telling me that in his opinion Pound was one of the greatest poets who had ever lived and was always a generous and kind friend, but that for some years Pound's mental condition had not been normal in the opinion of Hemingway, Joyce and others.

Arrangements were made for Dr. Muncie to examine Pound, both privately and together with three government psychiatrists who were assigned to the case by Judge Laws: Dr. Winfred Overholser, head of St. Elizabeths Hospital in Washington, Dr. Marion R. King, head psychitrist of the United States Public Health Service, and Dr. Joseph L. Gilbert, head psychiatrist of the Gallinger Hospital in Washington.

The result of the examination astonished me. I had expected that the government's doctors would find Pound fit for trial in view of the fact that Army doctors at the military detention center in Pisa had found him sane enough and had sent him to the United States for trial. Furthermore, the government had brought over a plane load of Italian radio officials to testify against him. (Ironically, the witnesses spent several months in a resort hotel at Hot Springs, Virginia, enjoying a luxurious vacation at the American taxpayers' expense, only to be shipped back to Italy when the treason trial failed to come off.) In view of the elaborate preparations which had been made, I was greatly surprised when Dr. Muncie told me that all four doctors had agreed that Pound was mentally unfit for trial.

This turn of events was partly the result, I believe, of Dr. Overholser's insistence that four experienced psychiatrists should be able to reach an agreement about the condition of their patient and should not allow a sanity trial to develop into the usual farce where eminent psychiatrists on both sides of the case reach different results and leave to the jury a decision which should be made by the medical profession. Such a dispute between doctors, in Overholser's opinion, was unworthy of the profession, degrading to the doctors involved and a hindrance to the judicial process.

When the four doctors first met, therefore, Dr. Overholser told them that he hoped they would reach common agreement on the condition of the prisoner, objectively, without partisan bias in favor of the government or the defense.

After examining Pound in this spirit, the doctors had no difficulty in agreeing upon the diagnosis that Pound was suffering from a paranoid state which rendered him mentally unfit to advise properly with his counsel or to participate intelligently and reasonably in a trial and, therefore, he should not be tried but should be cared for in a mental hospital.

The doctors joined in a brief report to Judge Laws which was read by him in court December 21, 1945. Here are the medical report and a newspaper account of the scene in the courtroom.

REPORT OF PSYCHIATRIC EXAMINATION

Sir:

The undersigned hereby respectfully report the results of their mental examination of Ezra Pound, now detained in Gallinger Hospital by transfer for observation from the District Jail on a charge of treason. Three of us (Drs. Gilbert, King, and Overholser) were appointed by your Honor to make this examination. At our suggestion, and with your approval, Dr. Wendell Muncie, acting upon the request of counsel for the accused, made an examination with us and associates himself with us in this joint report. Dr. Muncie spent several hours with the defendant, both alone and with us, on December 13, 1945, and the others of us have examined the defendant each on several occasions, separately and together, in the period from his admission to Gallinger Hospital on December 4, 1945 to December 13, 1945. We have had available to us the reports of laboratory, psychological and special physical examinations of the defendant and considerable material in the line of his writings and biographical data.

The defendant, now 60 years of age and in generally good physical condition, was a precocious student, specializing in literature. He has been a voluntary expatriate for nearly 40 years, living in England and France, and for the past 21 years in Italy, making an uncertain living by writing poetry and criticism. His poetry and literary criticism have achieved considerable recognition, but of recent years his preoccupation with monetary theories and economics has apparently obstructed his literary productivity. He has long been recognized as eccentric, querulous, and egocentric.

At the present time he exhibits extremely poor judgment as to his situation, its seriousness and the manner in which the charges are to be met. He insists that his broadcasts were not treasonable, but that all of his radio activities have stemmed from his self-appointed mission to "save the Constitution." He is abnormally grandiose, is expansive and exuberant in manner, exhibiting pressure of speech, discursiveness, and distractibility. In our opinion, with advancing years his personality, for many years abnormal, has undergone further distortion to the extent that he is now suffering from a paranoid state which renders him mentally unfit to advise properly with counsel or to participate intelligently and reasonably in his own defense. He is, in other words, insane and mentally unfit for trial, and is in need of care in a mental hospital.

Respectfully submitted,

JOSEPH L. GILBERT, M.D.
MARION R. KING, M.D.
WENDELL MUNCIE, M.D.
WINFRED OVERHOLSER, M.D.

NEW YORK HERALD TRIBUNE, DECEMBER 22, 1945

WASHINGTON, Dec. 21, 1945.—Ezra Pound, the American-born poet accused of treason, was declared today to be "insane and mentally unfit for trial" by a board of four psychiatrists, and was ordered removed to Washington's St. Elizabeths Hospital for the Insane by a Federal District Court here.

The government's prosecuting attorneys, however, said they would demand a public insanity hearing and pointed out that immediately before Pound left an Army Prison camp in Italy a month ago Army psychiatrists examined him and found him sane.

The District of Columbia psychiatrists, who made their report to Chief Justice Bolitha Laws, said they found Pound "mentally unfit to advise properly with counsel or to participate intelligently and reasonably in his own defense." They described the poet as "abnormally grandiose, expansive and exuberant in manner."

Accused of nineteen overt acts of treason for expounding Fascist propaganda against this country over the Rome radio, Pound has been in Gallinger Hospital here for observation since Nov. 27, when, during his arraignment for treason, he stood mute, on ground of his mental condition.

On the basis of their study, the psychiatrists reported that Pound's Fascist radio activities stemmed from what was termed a "self-appointed mission to save the Constitution."

Julien Cornell, of New York, Pound's defense attorney at the original arraignment, suggested that the poet's condition was largely a result of treatment he received at the Army prison camp. The sixty-year-old prisoner had been kept "incommunicado" in a small iron cage for seven months, he said. * * *

Prosecuting attorneys, however, said they believed Pound, like Rudolf Hess, might easily be feigning insanity to escape a trial that might cost his life. For that reason, they said, they would request a public insanity hearing. The prosecutors said Army psychiatrists thought Pound might be suffering from claustrophobia, but that it was a temporary condition, and that in other respects, except for his usual eccentricity, the prisoner was sane and able to stand trial for treason.

Psychiatrists making today's report included Dr. Joseph L. Gilbert, Dr. Marion R. King, Dr. Wendell Muncie and Dr. Winfred Overholser, superintendent of St. Elizabeths Hospital.

In addition to the problem of getting Pound released to a hospital for treatment, I was faced with financial difficulties because of wartime restrictions on the transfer of funds. Mrs. Pound had funds in England which were blocked by the British government. Pound himself had an account in a bank in Pennsylvania which had been blocked by the Alien Property Custodian. I took steps to try to have these funds released, but there did not appear to be much prospect of this being done. Meanwhile expenses were mounting, Dr. Muncie's fee had to be paid and I had incurred expense for a number of trips to Washington.

The immediate financial problem was met quite unexpectedly. On November 29, 1945, I called upon the poet E. E. Cummings and his wife at their home on Patchin Place in Greenwich Village. They expressed great concern over their old friend Ezra Pound and asked me about his condition and the legal predicament in which he found himself. Among other things, I told them about the blocking of his funds. As I was about to take my leave, Cummings walked over to a desk in a corner of the room and fished out a check for $1,000 drawn to his order by an art gallery. He presented me with the check, saying, "I sold a painting last week and don't need the money. Please take it and and use it for Ezra."

I was much surprised and moved by this spontaneous generosity. I told Cummings that I would use this money for medical and hospital expenses. Later on, when Mrs. Pound's funds were released, she insisted upon repaying Cummings, although he had intended a gift rather than a loan.

V

THE TRIAL

WHEN JUDGE LAWS ORDERED POUND TRANSFERRED to St. Elizabeths Hospital, under the Federal statute which requires the confinement in that institution of all Federal prisoners under indictment who are found to be unable to stand trial because of lack of competence or understanding, he was placed in the prison ward, known as Howard Hall, a grim building with locked doors and gratings at the windows. Outside the building there was an exercise yard surrounded by a very high wall. Like the other prisoners, Pound was allowed a brief daily period of exercise in the yard but at other times was locked in. He found the confinement intolerable. The claustrophobia which had come over him in Pisa now returned.

Perhaps because of the publicity which the case was receiving, the Department of Justice was not content to allow Pound to remain at St. Elizabeths indefinitely without a public trial. There was continuing clamor in the newspapers about Pound. Many people claimed that he was merely a fascist and no more insane than any other fascist. I believe that much of the bitterness against him derived from the anti-Semitic tone of some of his broadcasts from Rome. There was one newspaper reporter, Albert Deutsch, who took a special interest in the matter and wrote at length in the newspapers in an unfriendly vein. He apparently had had considerable experience in psychiatric matters and tried to convince everyone that Pound was sane and fit to be tried. He even suggested to Matlack that he should adopt the line of argument that Pound's insanity was no different from the insanity of other war criminals and traitors.

This was the state of affairs when the Department of Justice requested Judge Laws to order a jury trial. I had no objection and the judge so ordered. This development was reported to Mrs. Pound in the following letter:

LETTER FROM JULIEN CORNELL TO DOROTHY POUND

January 25, 1946

Dear Mrs. Pound:

I have your letter of December 8th. Your husband's address is St. Elizabeths Hospital, Washington, D. C. You can write to him directly in the future. Meanwhile, I have given him your message.

There is to be a formal hearing next week on the question of whether his mental condition would permit him to stand trial. The result is a foregone conclusion since all the doctors are in agreement that he is in no condition to be tried and requires hospital treatment. However, this proceeding is a formality which the law requires.

I have learned from questioning the doctors that they do not anticipate any substantial change in your husband's condition and also that they do not think he needs to remain very long in a hospital. I expect, therefore, that after a few months the case will be dropped and he will be set free.

You need not be alarmed about the report on your husband's mental condition. While, no doubt, his difficulties were aggravated by the ordeal of his imprisonment, he has been resting comfortably in a hospital for some time now, and I believe that his condition is just about normal. However, a state which would, no doubt, appear to you to be normal, is defined by the doctors as paranoid in character, to an extent which impairs your husband's judgment of his predicament and renders him unable to properly defend himself.

While the doctors are agreed that he is to this extent mentally abnormal, I feel quite sure that you will find, when you see him again, that he is his usual self, and the mental aberrations which the doctors have found are not anything new or unusual, but are chronic and would pass entirely unnoticed by one like yourself who has lived close to him for a number of years. In fact I think it may be fairly said that any man of his genius would be regarded by a psychiatrist as abnormal.

I am sorry that you may have been startled and alarmed by reports of your husband's condition and I hope that you can understand that he may appear to a stranger in quite a different way from the way in which he appears to you. Those who have known him for some time, such as James Laughlin, tell me that he is very much his old self, and I feel confident, therefore, that you need have no worry. On the other hand, you may rejoice that we have found a way to get around the difficulties presented by the indictment against him, and that these difficulties are all but surmounted.

Sincerely yours,

JULIEN CORNELL

Why was a sanity hearing necessary? Four eminent psychiatrists had already found Pound unfit to stand trial. When they re-examined him after some months of hospitalization they found no change in his mental condition, although he had recovered from the state of physical exhaustion in which I found him when he first arrived here. In view of the fuss which had been made over the Pound case, the first treason trial of the war, with a plane load of witnesses brought from Italy and public clamor for vengeance to be inflicted upon the "traitor," it is no wonder that the Department of Justice, although doubtless convinced that Pound was unfit to be tried, felt that they had to have a public trial of the issue. Matlack and Anderson, the government's lawyers, knew just as well as I did what the outcome would be, because the reports from St. Elizabeths were that Pound's condition was unchanged since the previous psychiatric examination.

But there was one thing which I knew that the government's lawyers did not know.

The day before the trial I went to the hospital to see Pound and prepare him for the ordeal of appearing in court. After explaining to him what was going to happen, I stopped in Dr. Overholser's office to pay my respects.

Dr. Overholser asked me to wait a moment, as he wanted to talk to me. When I was ushered into his private office he told me abruptly that he wished to disclose something to me which he had not told Matlack and was not going to tell him. This was a great surprise to me, as Overholser was the government's "star witness" who would not ordinarily volunteer any information to the defense attorney, much less information which he had not disclosed to the prosecution. But Overholser, as I had already found out, was a most unusual man.

He told me that he remained firm in his opinion that Pound was mentally unfit to stand trial, but, he said, many of the young doctors on his staff disagreed. They thought Pound was merely eccentric, and wanted to see him tried and convicted. Overholser felt they were in error, perhaps their judgment was distorted by patriotism, but however that might be, Overholser was the responsible official, he had reviewed the opinions of his juniors, and remained unshaken in his own opinion. I asked him what he would say if the prosecution inquired about the views of the other doctors. He answered that he would take their reports with him to the courtroom in his briefcase, and if necessary would read them to the court and explain why he disagreed.

Since the four doctors who had examined Pound were most eminent men, and three of them were government officials, I had no doubt that the opposing opinions of the young doctors on Overholser's staff would not carry much if any weight with the court. Still, it was an odd situation, where the chief witness for the government was telling the defense attorney about evidence which was not going to be disclosed to the prosecution unless they asked for it.

At one point during the trial, one of the government's lawyers did ask Overholser if he had received opinions about Pound from his staff, and he answered that he had the reports in his briefcase and could produce them. But he was not asked to do so. I smiled to myself at Dr. Overholser's confidence and daring.

It would not have made any difference anyway, if the conflicting reports of the young doctors had been read, as they would have been far outweighed by the opinions of Overholser, King, Gilbert and Muncie, who expressed not the slightest doubt in their view that Pound was not sufficiently sane to stand trial, and never would be.

The trial itself was well publicized and well attended. Laughlin was there. So was Albert Deutsch, the newspaper man I have mentioned, and a large number of other reporters.

I was somewhat worried about Pound. He was very nervous about the trial and I was afraid he might blow up. I told him that I would not put him on the witness stand, and he did not need to do anything but listen to the proceedings.

Despite my efforts to calm my client's anxiety, he did make one outburst, when Matlack in questioning one of the doctors characterized Pound as a fascist. Pound instantly jumped to his feet and shouted in a thunderous voice, "I never did believe in fascism, God damn it, I am opposed to fascism." Then he slumped again to his seat.

Judge Laws refused my request to direct a verdict, although I felt that the evidence was conclusive in favor of the defendant, but charged the jury in such a way that it took them only five minutes to bring in a verdict that Pound was mentally unfit to be tried.

The stenographic transcript of the trial is given in full in an appendix.

NEW YORK HERALD TRIBUNE, FEBRUARY 14, 1946

WASHINGTON, Feb. 13, 1946.—The treason case against Ezra Pound, expatriate American poet, was pigeon-holed today when a specially impaneled Federal jury returned a verdict that Pound is "mentally unsound" and unfit to stand trial on treason charges arising out of his war-time writings and broadcasts in Fascist Italy. This is the first time an accused war criminal has escaped trial because of insanity.

The sixty-year-old poet will be confined here at the St. Elizabeths Federal Hospital for the Insane. He may again face trial if he recovers from his present "paranoiac state," government prosecutors said, pointing out that a treason charge has no limitation, being valid until the defendant dies. They virtually conceded defeat, however, by announcing that the government will send back to Italy seven Fascist radio announcers who were to have been key witnesses against Pound.

The jury deliberated only five minutes after hearing four and a half hours' testimony by four psychiatrists. Chief Justice Bolitha

Laws, of the Federal District Court hearing the case, called the jury at the request of the prosecution.

The same psychiatrists had filed affidavits with the court on Dec. 14 declaring the poet unfit for trial, but government attorneys had demanded a public jury hearing of their findings. The four witnesses were Drs. Wendell Muncie, of the John Hopkins University psychiatry school; Marion R. King, medical director and psychiatrist of the Federal Bureau of Prisons; Winfred Overholser, superintendent of St. Elizabeths, and Joseph L. Gilbert, superintendent of the psychopathic ward, Gallinger Hospital here. All four experts agreed that Pound is mentally unsound, probably permanently. They all attested a prevailing "grandiosity" in the poet, which they said indicated his abnormal mental state.

Pound was not called to testify, but he sprang to his feet at one point, shouting, "I've never been a Fascist, Goddamit! I've always opposed them." He did this when a government attorney asked a witness if he had ever heard Pound speak of his views on Fascism.

Throughout the rest of the hearing, the bearded defendant moved nervously in his seat, held his head in his hands or leaned back and stared at the ceiling.

The psychiatrists reported that nearly two months' observation of Pound's mental condition revealed a number of "fixed ideas" held by the poet: That his mission in life was to save the United States Constitution, that the only way to world peace was through the teachings of Confucius, that he could have prevented the formation of the Axis and the war by uniting intellectual groups of the world and that he was persecuted by bureaucrats.

All four agreed that, in their observation, Pound was not able to explain his reasons for holding these views, and that he could not confer logically on any subject for even a brief period. They said they believed, therefore, that he would not be able to consult with his counsel on defense against the treason charges.

VI

HABEAS CORPUS

By Federal statute, a person under indictment for a crime who is found mentally unable to stand trial must be confined at St. Elizabeths Hospital, which is situated in the outskirts of Washington. Under this statute, Pound was returned after the hearing to St. Elizabeths Hospital, there to be confined indefinitely unless his condition should improve sufficiently to permit him to be tried. This, the doctors told me, would never happen. Thus Pound found himself, in effect, under a sentence of life imprisonment despite the fact that he was innocent in the eyes of the law. This peculiar legal paradox is discussed in this chapter.

There are many buildings at St. Elizabeths, spread over extensive grounds with pleasant lawns, shaded walks and recreational facilities. Patients who are under the jurisdiction of the criminal courts are kept in a separate building where they are closely guarded. As mentioned above, Pound had found his close confinement almost unbearable.

Now that he was no longer awaiting trial and there was little likelihood that he would ever be tried, there seemed no reason to keep him locked up in a cell, but it was the policy of the hospital to keep under guard all persons accused of crime. Nevertheless, I was able to persuade Dr. Overholser, with the approval of the Department of Justice and Judge Laws, to remove Pound from the prison ward of the hospital to the main building where he had much more freedom of movement and eventually he was allowed to stroll about the grounds with his wife. Although Pound was a prisoner, the doctor felt that there was no danger of his trying to escape and that keeping him in the prison ward was both harmful and unnecessary. Pound was grateful for being allowed to leave the prison ward and found life at St. Elizabeths thereafter as tolerable as life can be under such circumstances.

Already I had been giving consideration to ways and means of having Pound released, because there seemed no possibility that he would ever be tried and his illness was so mild that he did not need hospitalization.

A letter which I wrote to Mr. Moore about this situation and his reply are as follows:

LETTER FROM JULIEN CORNELL TO ARTHUR V. MOORE

March 4, 1946

Dear Mr. Moore:

I presume that you received the news which I sent you by cable that Mr. Pound was found by a jury to be mentally unfit to stand trial and was again ordered by the court to be committed to St. Elizabeths Hospital in Washington, D. C. This result followed an all day hearing, held at the request of the government, at which four eminent psychiatrists gave testimony to the effect that because of a mental condition which makes it impossible for him to reason logically or discuss intelligently his predicament, Mr. Pound is unable to understand clearly or to consult with counsel concerning the questions which would be involved in a trial, and is therefore unable to conduct properly his defense. I will not attempt to characterize further the medical testimony since I have ordered a transcript from the court stenographer and will shortly send you excerpts from the record of the actual proceedings.

Although this fact was not in issue at the hearing, the doctors appear to be agreed that the possibility is very remote that Mr. Pound will ever be able to stand trial. Although his family and friends would probably find his condition a normal one, I am inclined to believe that the abnormalities which the doctors found in Mr. Pound's mental processes, while they may have been aggravated by recent fear and worry, are deep rooted and have existed for a long time. I think it unlikely that there will be any considerable change in the future.

If this prognosis proves to be correct, I would recommend that an attempt be made to have Mr. Pound released from the hospital, although I expect that it will be impossible to have the indictment dismissed since the government will want to preserve the right to bring him to trial if his condition should at any time permit this to be done.

This may raise intricate and novel legal questions since the statute under which Mr. Pound has been committed to the hospital provides only that a person who is unable to stand trial because of a mental condition shall be committed to a hospital and may at any time be returned to the jurisdiction of the court if the mental difficulties are overcome. The statute does not apparently contemplate release from the hospital if the mental condition proves to be permanent and the welfare of the patient and the safety of the public would permit him to be discharged. The statute probably reflects an outmoded view of insanity under which all insane persons were regarded as dangerous maniacs who needed to be shut up in institutions, while many persons mentally abnormal, whose behavior was not extraordinary, were not generally understood to be insane. Perhaps because of such lack of understanding of mental disorders, Congress failed to consider the possibility that a person might be unable to stand trial and yet not require permanent hospitalization. However, the statute does not expressly prohibit the discharge from a mental institution of a person under indictment. The trial judge would have discretion to order such discharge either with or without bond. It may prove difficult, however, to persuade a judge to do this since there appears to be no precedent for it and the statute apparently does not contemplate such an eventuality.

Not only does the trial judge in my opinion have discretion, in spite of the silence of the statute, to release Mr. Pound from the hospital, but even if the statute should be construed to prohibit such release, or if the judge should refuse to exercise his discretion, I think that Mr. Pound would have a constitutional right to be released if we can demonstrate that he is not going to be able ever to stand trial and that his welfare and public safety do not require hospitalization. If under such circumstances Mr. Pound were to be confined indefinitely in a hospital, this would be equivalent to incarceration, not because he required medical treatment, but solely because he is under indictment and unable to clear himself because of his mental condition. Although he still would be presumed innocent under the law, he would be incarcerated indefinitely, possibly for life, because the government had obtained an indictment against him. I feel confident that constitutional rights would be thereby violated and that the courts would order him to be set free. It might be necessary, however, to appeal such a case to the higher courts because a trial judge might be fearful to set a precedent in such a novel situation.

My advice is that after the expiration of several months, an opinion be sought from the Superintendent of St. Elizabeths Hospital, and possibly other psychiatrists, with regard to the questions mentioned above, and if the doctors are then of the opinion that Mr. Pound will never be able to stand trial and also that he does not require hospital treatment, an application should be made for a writ of habeas corpus to secure his release. I think that the government would either actively resist such an effort or would at least refuse to consent, and without the consent of the government, it is quite likely that a trial judge would be unwilling to assume the responsibility for releasing Mr. Pound and an appeal would become necessary. I think the expense of an appeal would be well worth while, since the prospects for gaining complete freedom would be favorable.

I should like to know whether you and Mrs. Pound agree with these suggestions and whether you would like me to continue along these lines.

Sincerely yours,

JULIEN CORNELL

LETTER FROM ARTHUR V. MOORE TO JULIEN CORNELL

March 12, 1946

Dear Mr. Cornell:

I duly received your cable informing me of the result of the trial, and I have since received your letter of the 4th instant with details of the hearing, for which I am much obliged, and may I say at once how very grateful I am to you for all you have done for Ezra Pound.

I confess I am not conversant with the process of American law, and I find your letter most enlightening.

It is quite evident the amount of work, time and trouble involved has been tremendous.

I have daily been expecting to receive a telegram from Mrs. Pound to the effect that she was leaving Genoa for the United States, for I understand she has booked a passage, and is now awaiting a boat, and in fact may now be on her journey.

I am therefore unable to let you know whether she agrees to your suggestions for future procedure, and would suggest that you wait until she can see you personally to give you her instructions. I am of the opinion that we should not be in too great hurry to press for the dismissal of the indictment, for I understand there is still some agitation and a campaign against Mr. Pound going on in the New York paper "P.M."

Yours sincerely,

ARTHUR V. MOORE

Born a British subject, Dorothy Shakespear Pound lost her British citizenship when she married an American. Having lived all her life in Europe, and Pound himself having been domiciled there for forty years, Mrs. Pound let her American passport lapse, and when her husband was brought to the United States for trial she found herself unable to follow him. It was not until June, 1946, that Mrs. Pound was able to get her passport renewed and sailed from Genoa on the S. S. *Marine Carp.*

Left behind in Rapallo was Pound's aged mother* and his daughter Mary, who later married the Egyptologist, Prince Boris de Rachewiltz. They have two children, grandchildren of Ezra Pound, with whom they live in an ancient castle near Merano in the Italian Alps.

---

* Isabel Weston Pound; his father Homer Loomis Pound died at Rapallo in 1942.

Mrs. Pound was put on a plane to Washington where she was met by the Mapel sisters, who had shown themselves to be such staunch friends of Pound. She was taken into their home until she could find a room within walking distance of St. Elizabeths where she could be near her husband.

Mrs. Pound's devotion to her husband was touching. She never questioned the rightness of his actions, nor complained about the rigors of her life in Washington, where she spent the next twelve years doing nothing but comfort and serve him, visiting him on every visiting day, taking him for walks on the grounds in fine weather, looking after his creature comforts and not least, attending to the throngs of visitors and correspondents who fastened themselves like leeches upon the great fish in his public fishbowl.

Soon after Mrs. Pound arrived in Washington, this correspondence ensued:

LETTER FROM DOROTHY POUND TO JULIEN CORNELL

July 14, 1946

Dear Mr. Cornell:

I have now seen Ezra three times—the first time for an hour. I find him very nervous and jumpy. I believe his wits are really very scattered, and he has difficulty in concentrating for more than a few minutes. During the one hour we spoke mostly of family odds and ends,—on Thursday of his Chinese translating chiefly, and I have introduced myself to the head of Ch. Dept. in Congressional Library who is much interested in Ezra's work. Today Ezra spoke of my trying to find out what was going on in the outside world. He has newspapers, but naturally hasn't much faith in that kind of news.

I met the mother of a young man E.P. has talked with in St. Elizabeths. She was full of the idea of "going to the Women of the P.E.N. Club, and making them ask the President for clemency". I said it was important to choose the right moment.

I do believe we must try to get Ezra *out* of that place. He himself says he'll never get well in there and has said so each time to me. He wants to know very much how far you understand the case. He does not feel, I rather gather, that you are "on to" all his economic learning. He has made the following statement to me—"Treason is not an extraditable offense".

When he gave himself up in May, 1945 he volunteered to go to the U.S.A. "to give information to the State Dept." instead of which they handcuffed him and took him to prison. He says in passing that a man cannot be handcuffed in a moving vehicle.

What I am wondering is how can E. be gotten into a private sanatorium, less imprisoned, and if he left St. Elizabeths, would those four doctors still be in position to testify to his mental instability. What can be done as quickly as possible, in safety? He says he has had no contact with any "adult" mind. Of course 15 minutes makes a break—but that's all. T. S. Eliot evidently feels strongly he should be moved. I am writing to Laughlin by this post. What places are there? Dr. Overholser is still away.

The Misses Mapel so very kind and helpful.

Sincerely yours,

DOROTHY POUND

LETTER FROM JULIEN CORNELL TO DOROTHY POUND

July 15, 1946

Dear Mrs. Pound:

This is in reply to your letter of July 14th. I am sure you are right that your husband would be much better off in a private sanatorium. However, I do not think that the present is an opportune time to make an application to the court for his removal. This could be done only by the granting of bail or the dismissal of the charges. I discussed this question with Mr. Eliot, Mr. Laughlin and others a few weeks ago and all were agreed that such an application should not be made at the present time because of public clamor which would arise in opposition.

In my opinion we should wait before making application for your husband's release from St. Elizabeths, at least until the fall, unless, perhaps, Dr. Overholser could be persuaded to testify that the state of his health required removal to a private sanatorium. If Dr. Overholser recommends it, then I think the judge might be willing to grant bail for that purpose. I suggest that you try to see Dr. Overholser about this and I shall attempt to see him within the next few weeks also.

I think your husband can rest assured that I have a pretty good understanding of the entire case including his economic theories and the motives underlying his broadcasts. I have made it a point to study not only his poetry but his economic tracts and I have read up on Social Credit in general.

Sincerely yours,

JULIEN CORNELL

LETTER FROM DOROTHY POUND TO JULIEN CORNELL

July 17, 1946

Dear Mr. Cornell:

Thanks for your letter of July 15th., and for your word, which I have passed on to Ezra about your "understanding of the entire case". I wanted something to reassure him a little. I think he feels he is put aside and forgotten. He asks me to write certain letters for him each time I go there and I do my best. I am most anxious to see Dr. Overholser to find out about *which way* to treat him on certain subjects. He (E.P.) is certainly very nervous and worried.

I have been through the pile of doctors' testimony—very interesting. I should like to keep it awhile and re-read it when I have a little more leisure. I am hoping I may find a room near the hospital for myself.

Yours very sincerely,

DOROTHY POUND

As mentioned previously, it was my opinion that Pound could not be kept under confinement indefinitely, merely because he had been indicted, if there appeared no reasonable possibility that he could be brought to trial. This would amount to life imprisonment of a man who was presumed to be innocent, but the Federal statutes did not contain any provision for his release and this precise question had never been tested in the courts. It was, therefore, my plan to seek a writ of habeas corpus to determine whether Pound should be kept indefinitely confined or released.

I planned my attack on broad constitutional grounds, fully expecting that a District Judge would probably not be willing to establish a precedent and that the question would have to be carried on appeal to the Circuit Court of Appeals and probably to the United States Supreme Court. Despite the novelty of the issue and anticipating firm objections from the Department of Justice, I nevertheless felt confident that I could succeed if I could get the case before the Supreme Court.

My first step, prior to the habeas corpus proceeding, was to make a renewed application for bail. Mrs. Pound had not wanted anything to be done until after the elections of November 1946. Then I wrote to Pound telling him that I was going to try to have him released on bail because Dr. Overholser did not think his confinement was necessary and in my opinion he should not be kept incarcerated unless there was some reasonable prospect of his being tried. My letter to Pound and motion which I presented to the District Court asking for bail, together with a letter to Mrs. Pound and a letter to Laughlin explaining the outcome, follow:

LETTER FROM JULIEN CORNELL TO EZRA POUND

November 7, 1946

Dear Ezra Pound:

Now that the elections are over I am proceeding as planned to make application for your release since all concerned seem to be agreed that this is the most opportune time.

The question is an unusual one and presents some legal difficulties which may make it necessary to appeal, but I am convinced that you have a constitutional right to be released if your own health and the interests of society do not require that you be confined. I do not believe that a man can be shut up indefinitely after being indicted when he cannot be tried because of illness.

You are presumed to be innocent until proved otherwise, and since there is no prospect that you can ever be proved guilty, you cannot in my opinion be indefinitely confined merely because of the indictment.

Sincerely yours,

JULIEN CORNELL

MOTION FOR BAIL HEARD JANUARY 29, 1947

Comes now the defendant by his counsel, JULIEN CORNELL, and moves the court for an order admitting the defendant to bail and for the grounds of this motion respectfully shows:

1. The defendant was indicted for treason on November 26, 1945 in the District of Columbia.

2. Upon his arraignment on November 27, 1945 the defendant was transferred to Gallinger Hospital by order of this court for psychiatric examination by Drs. Winfred Overholser, Marion L. King, Joseph L. Gilbert and Wendell Muncie. They reported to the court on December 14, 1945 their unanimous opinion that the defendant was mentally unfit for trial and in need of care in a mental hospital.

3. On December 21, 1945, the defendant's motion for bail was heard and denied and it was ordered that the defendant be sent to St. Elizabeths Hospital for treatment and examination. He has since been continuously confined at St. Elizabeths Hospital.

4. Subsequent to the defendant's commitment to St. Elizabeths Hospital, the court ordered a formal jury trial on the question of his sanity upon motion by the United States. At such trial on February 13, 1946, after testimony by the four psychiatrists mentioned above that he then was and had for many years been insane, the defendant was found by the court and a jury to be of unsound mind and therefore unfit for trial and was remanded to St. Elizabeths Hospital.

5. The defendant has been continuously in custody charged with treason since early in May 1945. He was held at a military prison at Pisa, Italy, until he was brought by plane to Washington, D. C. where he arrived on November 18, 1945. He has thus been incarcerated for more than a year in the United States and for an additional six months in Italy.

6. Defendant's attorney has been informed by Dr. Winfred Overholser, Superintendent of St. Elizabeths Hospital, based upon his examination and treatment of the defendant which covers a period of about one year beginning at about the time of his admission to Gallinger Hospital on December 4, 1945, that in his opinion

(1) the defendant has been insane for many years and will never recover his sanity or become mentally fit to stand trial on the indictment (2) the defendant's mental condition is not benefited by his close confinement at St. Elizabeths Hospital where he is kept in a building with violent patients because of the necessity for keeping him under guard, and it would be desirable from the point of view of the health and welfare of the defendant if he could be removed to a private sanatorium and (3) the defendant is not violent, does not require close confinement and the public safety would not be impaired if he were allowed the degree of liberty which a private sanatorium permits for patients who are mildly insane.

7. It therefore appears from Dr. Overholser's opinion, based upon a full year of observation and treatment, that the defendant can never be brought to trial on this indictment and will for the rest of his life be presumed innocent in law, although he may remain under the charge of treason. It appears also from the medical standpoint that the continuance of his present incarceration is not desirable and his transfer to a private sanatorium would benefit him.

8. If on medical grounds the defendant should be released from custody, then to continue to hold him would be equivalent to a sentence of life imprisonment upon a man who is and always will be presumed innocent. He would be confined for the rest of his life because of an accusation which can never be proved. It is respectfully submitted that such confinement would be unlawful and unconstitutional.

9. Congress has provided that when a person charged with crime is found to be insane and unable to stand trial he may be confined in St. Elizabeths Hospital (24 U. S. C. Sec. 211). It is further provided that if such a person is restored to sanity he shall be returned to the court for trial (24 U. S. C. Sec. 211b). The law is silent, however, as to what should be done with a person who having been sent to St. Elizabeths Hospital is determined to be permanently insane but not to require permanent hospitalization.

10. Although the statute is silent on the point, if it should be construed so as to prevent release from St. Elizabeths Hospital of a person like the defendant who is found to be permanently insane,

but not requiring hospitalization, then the statute would be unconstitutional. In the absence of medical grounds, a man may not be subjected to life imprisonment because an unprovable accusation has been brought against him. He would then be deprived of liberty without due process of law in violation of the Fifth Amendment to the United States Constitution.

11. It is respectfully submitted that based upon the medical opinions above referred to the defendant has a legal and constitutional right to be released from custody. If there is doubt as to the accuracy of medical opinion that he will never be restored to sanity, the court may retain control over the defendant by admitting him to bail and placing him in the care of a responsible physician. Bail is expressly permitted even in capital offenses (18 U. S. C. Sec. 597). It is therefore respectfully requested that the defendant be ordered released from St. Elizabeths Hospital and be admitted to bail and placed in the care of a private physician approved by the court.

JULIEN CORNELL
Attorney for Defendant

LETTER FROM JULIEN CORNELL TO JAMES LAUGHLIN

February 10, 1947

Dear J:

You will be interested to know the outcome of my application for Ezra's release to a private hospital. Dr. Overholser was summoned to court and testified that Ezra would be benefited by removal from Howard Hall where he is much restricted in his privileges and surrounded by criminally insane, but he said that he needed further hospitalization and could be as well cared for in St. Elizabeths as anywhere else. Accordingly, we agreed upon a compromise under which the Judge and the Attorney General have consented to have Ezra removed to a more comfortable part of St. Elizabeths, thereby relieving Dr. Overholser from a responsibility which he would not have otherwise assumed. It is an inflexible rule of the hospital to keep patients under indictment in Howard Hall which is the only completely guarded building. The enclosed letter from Dorothy indicates that she and Ezra are both happy over the new arrangement.

Best regards,

JULIEN

Mrs. Pound had written me that her husband had moved to his new quarters February 4th, where he had a room to himself with a view of the Potomac instead of the barred cell at Howard Hall, and Mrs. Pound had been able to visit him for two hours instead of the "terrible fifteen minutes" allowed in the criminal ward.

It was nearly a year later that I wrote to Mrs. Pound urging her to authorize me to try to have Pound released under a writ of habeas corpus. She agreed that he should be gotten out if at all possible and I prepared a habeas corpus petition. Here is my correspondence on the subject with Mrs. Pound:

LETTER FROM JULIEN CORNELL TO DOROTHY POUND

December 15, 1947

Dear Mrs. Pound:

As I told you on Wednesday, Dr. Overholser is firmly of the opinion that (1) there is no reasonable possibility that your husband will improve sufficiently that he could be tried and (2) there is no necessity for confinement in an institution.

I am sorry that I did not have an opportunity on Wednesday to discuss the future. I believe that we have a good chance of securing your husband's release from custody, although I know of no legal means by which the State Department could be compelled to issue a passport permitting his return to Italy. There may be a long struggle ahead of us. I would propose to tackle first the Department of Justice and the State Department in an effort to persuade them to drop the case and permit your husband to leave the country. If this proves unavailing, we would have to begin legal action and because of the novelty of the question and the serious nature of the alleged crime, it would probably be necessary to take the case up to the higher courts. Before we undertake such an effort, I think you should be perfectly clear as to your plans. If your husband is released, you will have a much heavier responsibility, and if you take him to Italy, you will have still greater burdens. I feel sure that your husband would be much happier if the restrictions of the institution were removed, and I know that you are anxious to get him out. Before attempting to have him released, however, I think you should decide just exactly where you will go, what you will do, and when. Your husband said yesterday that he would not want to go back to Italy before next spring. Do you share that thought?

I suggest that you consider the entire situation. In raising these points, I have no desire to suggest what your decision should be, but I think it would be helpful if you would give careful thought to the entire situation before I see you again. We can then discuss future plans and I am prepared to undertake any legal action which may seem advisable.

Sincerely yours,

JULIEN CORNELL

LETTER FROM DOROTHY POUND TO JULIEN CORNELL

December 18, 1947

Dear Mr. Cornell:

Ezra should be gotten out of custody. We have been talking it over. Italy seems very unquiet just now. We should prefer not to go back there for possibly 3-4 months—but we could find somewhere in Virginia or N. Carolina to go to on his release.

Difficult without knowing what conditions, or any? attached to release: local laws might need to be consulted also. I don't count he'll be able to earn any money. Small sums in royalties come in.

There is a possible alternative, of going to Spain. He speaks Spanish well. Have you any idea of the whereabouts of Amprim?

I understand he found nothing in the radio talks to be construed as treason.

It is to me incredible, you as E.P.'s lawyer, should not have access to the speeches.

Saluti cordiali and best wishes for 1948.

Let us know if you can before your next visit.

DOROTHY POUND

LETTER FROM JULIEN CORNELL TO DOROTHY POUND

February 9, 1948

Dear Mrs. Pound:

I have completed a petition for your husband's release which I want to discuss with the head of the Criminal Division of the Department of Justice, a Mr. Quinn,* whom I happen to know from the time when he was in charge of the Criminal Division of the United States Attorney's office in the Eastern District of New York. He is an amiable and reasonable individual, and I feel confident that he will be cooperative.

At the same time I should like to see you and get your signature on the petition.

Sincerely yours,

JULIEN CORNELL

The habeas corpus proceeding raised completely novel questions of law. As I expected, the writ was denied by the District Judge and I filed an immediate appeal, but Mrs. Pound apparently got "cold feet" about having her husband released and asked me to drop the appeal.

I explained to her that even if we should succeed in having her husband discharged from custody, there was no way to compel the Department of State to give him a passport to return to Italy. (The power of the Department of State to withhold a passport was at this time absolute. Not until many years later was this power broken by the United States Supreme Court.) I could therefore give Mrs. Pound no assurance that there was any likelihood of her husband

* T. Vincent Quinn.

being allowed to leave the country. His passport had been taken up and I doubted very much if he would be given another one. Their stay in the United States had been a bitter experience for both Mr. and Mrs. Pound. They longed to return to their home in Rapallo. But if they could not go back to Italy, Pound did not care very much about being released. He told me that if he had to remain in the United States, St. Elizabeths was probably as good a place for him as any.

Mrs. Pound never told me just why she decided to drop the appeal in the habeas corpus proceeding, but I believe her main reason was that she was not free to return home with her husband. Then too, she may have been fearful of the problem of shielding Pound both from his enemies and from his well-wishers if he should be released in her custody.

The habeas corpus petition is given here in full, with my letter to Mrs. Pound about its denial, and her reply.

PETITION FOR WRIT OF HABEAS CORPUS FILED IN UNITED STATES DISTRICT COURT FOR THE DISTRICT OF COLUMBIA, FEBRUARY 11, 1948

NOW comes Dorothy Pound, as Committee of the person and estate of Ezra Pound, an incompetent person, and in behalf of Ezra Pound petitions this court as follows:

1. Petitioner is a citizen of the United States, domiciled in Italy, and temporarily sojourning in the District of Columbia, and is the wife of Ezra Pound.

2. On October 30, 1946, the petitioner was appointed by the District Court for the District of Columbia, Committee of the person and estate of Ezra Pound, who had been adjudged a person of unsound mind, and petitioner has duly qualified and is now acting as such Committee.

3. The petitioner asks for the issuance of a Writ of Habeas Corpus to determine the legality of the detention of Ezra Pound in the custody of the respondent, Winfred Overholser, at St. Elizabeths Hospital, which is situated within the jurisdiction of this

court and is under the direction of the respondent who is Superintendent thereof.

4. Ezra Pound is a United States citizen, domiciled in Italy, and has been confined in the District of Columbia since November 18, 1945, under indictment on the charge of treason against the United States. He was first confined in the District of Columbia jail, but was removed for medical examination to Gallinger Hospital, at the request of his attorney, Julien Cornell, under order of this court dated November 27, 1945, which provided for an examination in regard to his sanity. Such examination was held and a report rendered to this court dated December 14, 1945, by the respondent and by Drs. Joseph L. Gilbert and Marion R. King, both appointed by the court for making such examination, and by Dr. Wendell Muncie, employed by my husband's attorney, in which all four physicians joined in the opinion that my husband was of unsound mind and mentally unfit to advise properly with counsel, or to participate intelligently or reasonably in the defense of the charge of treason, and he was in need of care in a mental hospital. Following such report it was ordered by this court on December 21, 1945, that my husband, Ezra Pound, be sent to St. Elizabeths Hospital for treatment and examination, and he was forthwith removed to St. Elizabeths Hospital where he has since been continuously confined.

5. On January 18, 1946, this court, upon motion of the United States, ordered that a hearing be held to determine the sanity of Ezra Pound, in connection with the indictment for treason pending against him. The hearing was held on February 13, 1946, and medical testimony was received from Drs. Overholser, Gilbert, King and Muncie above mentioned who reported that they had again examined my husband and on the basis of such examination and the previous examination, as well as observation of him in the interval, they all expressed the opinion that he was suffering from insanity of a paranoid type, which was of long duration, and that he would be unable properly to defend himself against the charge of treason, or to consult with counsel in his defense. At the conclusion of the testimony, a jury rendered a verdict that Ezra Pound was of unsound mind, and he was found by the court to be of unsound mind and remanded to St. Elizabeths Hospital.

6. On January 3, 1947, a motion was made by my husband's counsel for his admission to bail in order that he might be released from St. Elizabeths Hospital and privately treated. This motion was heard and denied by this court on January 29, 1947.

7. For a period of more than two years my husband has been under observation and treatment by the respondent, Dr. Winfred Overholser and his associates at St. Elizabeths Hospital. I know of my own knowledge and am informed by Dr. Overholser that such treatment has not resulted in any improvement in my husband's mental condition. Dr. Overholser informs me that in his opinion my husband will never recover his sanity, and there is no reasonable possibility that he will ever become mentally fit to stand trial.

8. In view of the fact that my husband appears to be permanently insane and can never be brought to trial under the indictment charging him with treason, I desire that he be released from St. Elizabeths Hospital and placed in my care. My attorney, Julien Cornell, has consulted with Dr. Overholser regarding the possibility of such release and has been informed by Dr. Overholser that in his opinion my husband does not require hospitalization; that his mental condition is of a mild nature which would permit him to be released from the hospital, and that he would benefit by the greater degree of freedom which would result from such release.

9. Although the respondent has expressed the opinion that my husband is permanently insane, and can never be brought to trial, and that he does not require hospitalization, the respondent, nevertheless, is unwilling and legally unable to release my husband from custody because he was committed to the respondent by order of this court.

10. If the court can rely upon Dr. Overholser's opinion, and he is not only eminently qualified to determine such matters, but has also had the opportunity to keep my husband under continuous observation for a period of more than two years, then it appears that my husband is being held in custody, not because his illness or public safety requires his confinement, but solely because of the indictment which has been issued against him.

11. My husband, Ezra Pound, is held in custody pursuant to the authority of Section 211 of Title 24 of the United States Code which provides as follows:

> "If any person, charged with crime, be found, in the court before which he is so charged, to be an insane person, such court shall certify the same to the Federal Security Administrator, who may order such person to be confined in Saint Elizabeths Hospital, and, if he be not indigent, he and his estate shall be charged with expenses of his support in the hospital."

12. The release from custody of persons so confined is provided in Section 211b of Title 24 of the United States Code which is as follows:

> "When any person confined in Saint Elizabeths Hospital charged with crime and subject to be tried therefor, or convicted of crime and undergoing sentence therefor, shall be restored to sanity, the superintendent of the hospital shall give notice thereof to the judge of the criminal court, and deliver him to the court in obedience to the proper precept."

13. There is no provision in the statutes for the release from custody of a person who is found to be permanently insane and consequently unable to be tried, yet whose mental condition does not require confinement in a hospital or asylum. The statute does not prohibit release of a person confined under such circumstances, but merely fails to make any provision to cover such an eventuality.

14. I am informed by counsel that my husband has the legal and constitutional right to be released from custody, because there is no justification in law for his continued confinement. When a person has been accused of crime and found to be of unsound mind, he may be properly confined for the reason that (1) there is an indictment pending against him under which he may be brought to trial if and when he recovers his sanity, or (2) his mental condition is such that he requires hospitalization, or (3) it would be dangerous to the public safety for him to remain at liberty. In the first case, the state is exercising its police power under which it may apprehend and confine persons awaiting trial while in the other cases the state is acting as the guardian and *parens patriae* of per-

sons who are unable to provide for their own welfare. But unless the state can properly bring to bear either its police power or its power of control over insane persons for the welfare of themselves and the general public, the state has no legal or constitutional right to hold in custody an insane person merely because he has been found to be insane. The Constitution still guarantees to him that his liberty shall not be taken away without due process of law, and if his own and the public welfare does not require it, he may not be deprived of his liberty by confinement in an institution. In the case of my husband, Ezra Pound, there is no reasonable possibility that he will recover his sanity, and, therefore, he can never be brought to trial under the indictment. It is also clear that his insanity is of a mild sort which does not require his continued hospitalization. Under these circumstances, if my husband is held indefinitely in confinement, he will in effect be confined for the rest of his life, solely because an indictment is pending against him which can never be resolved by trial.

15. It is a fundamental principle of law that every person is presumed to be innocent until he has been found guilty, and also that no person may be imprisoned until his guilt has been determined by due process of law. Under these principles, the indictment against my husband is no evidence of his guilt, and he must be presumed innocent of the charge against him, and such presumption will endure for the rest of his life, because he will never be in condition for trial. As a result, a presumably innocent man is being held in confinement and will be confined for life, merely because he has been charged with crime, and has not sufficient mental capacity to meet the charge. His confinement on such grounds is nowhere authorized by statute, or by any principle of law, and would deprive him of his liberty without due process of law in violation of the Fifth Amendment to the United States Constitution.

WHEREFORE, your petitioner prays that a Writ of Habeas Corpus be issued by this court directed to Dr. Winfred Overholser, Superintendent of St. Elizabeths Hospital, to produce the body of Ezra Pound before this court, at a time and place to be specified therein, then and there to receive and do what this court shall order concerning the detention and restraint of Ezra Pound, and that he shall be ordered to be discharged from the custody of the respondent and released to the care of the petitioner, as the Committee of his person and estate.

Dated: Washington, D. C.
February 11, 1948.

JULIEN CORNELL
Attorney for Petitioner

DOROTHY POUND
Petitioner

LETTER FROM JULIEN CORNELL TO DOROTHY POUND

March 4, 1948

Dear Mrs. Pound:

The District Court has refused to issue a writ of habeas corpus and I have filed an appeal. In making this decision the district judge must have assumed that the facts and opinions stated in the petition including the medical opinions could be substantiated, and he must have determined that even so, there would be insufficient grounds for your husband's release, otherwise he would have ordered a hearing at which evidence could be received to support the statements made in the petition.

I think there is a good chance to obtain a reversal on appeal. It seems to me that your husband obviously has the right to be released sooner or later if there is no medical reason for confining him. The case will not be an easy one, however, because there appears to be no precedent and also because of popular feeling against your husband's position which will be reflected to some extent in the attitude of the courts.

I want you to know that the appeal will be difficult, and that while I am confident in the justice of our position, victory is by no means assured. Unfortunately the courts are imperfect instruments and justice does not always prevail, particularly in cases which involve political emotions. I feel sure, however, that if the case is decided without intolerance and in accordance with legal principles, we should ultimately secure your husband's release.

If it is necessary to carry the case to the United States Supreme Court, we will probably not have a decision until next fall, but the intermediate appellate court should reach a decision within the next two or three months.

I shall keep you advised on further developments and will welcome any suggestions which may occur to you.

Sincerely yours,

JULIEN CORNELL

LETTER FROM DOROTHY POUND TO JULIEN CORNELL

March 13, 1948

Dear Mr. Cornell:

Your letter of March 11th received. Please withdraw the appeal at once. My husband is not fit to appear in court and must still be kept as quiet as possible; the least thing shakes his nerves up terribly. I want nothing attempted now until the November elections are over.

Sincerely,

DOROTHY POUND

I was gratified to learn later on that Thurman Arnold agreed with my view. He had been a professor at the Yale Law School when I was there and had been much liked and admired by me and by his other students. It was he who had been retained by Robert Frost to seek a pardon for Pound as discussed in Chapter VIII. In 1965 Arnold published a book about his legal career, *Fair Fights and Foul* in which he makes this comment about the habeas corpus situation on page 237:

> "To the increasing horror of the literary world here and abroad, Pound was detained in the criminal ward of St. Elizabeths for thirteen years. I seriously doubt if anyone in the Department of Justice wanted to keep him there. But there seemed no way of getting him out. The fact that he was too

mentally ill to be tried was not a reason for releasing him, because this had nothing to do with whether he was insane at the time of the offense. He could not be pardoned, because he was not convicted of any offense and there was nothing to pardon him for. He could not be tried and acquitted on the ground of insanity, because he refused to make that defense and, insane or not, the Supreme Court had held that he could not be forced to. It is my own opinion that had Mrs. Pound, acting as Pound's guardian, asked for habeas corpus on the ground that it was absurd to confine Pound for life because he could not be tried, she might have succeeded, though this had been tried once, and failed, in the lower court. So there was no way in conformity with the philosophical legal logic of the situation to release Pound except for the prosecution to dismiss the indictment."

VII

SAINT ELIZABETHS

PUBLIC INTEREST IN POUND remained unabated. With the benefit of hospital care and rest, he became much his old self and delighted in receiving visitors. He had a room to himself on the second floor of the main building of the hospital. Outside his door there were several tables and wicker chairs set up at the end of the corridor which Pound converted into a sort of sitting room where he received visitors. His wife spent an hour or more with him each day helping him to preside over his salon, or in fine weather sitting on a bench under the shade trees in view of guards but otherwise free and undisturbed. He even played an occasional set of tennis during the last year of his stay, a game in which he showed the same fire as in his poetry.

Pound's literary friends and many other people visited him at the hospital. He appeared to enjoy greatly the opportunity to talk with anyone who would listen, conversing at length on any subject which happened to come to mind. He also carried on a vigorous correspondence, as he had done all his life, and resumed the writing of his monumental "Cantos". The last section of the Cantos, composed in Pisa, showed in places the results of Pound's rigorous treatment at the hands of the army. Now that he had returned to his normal self, he was able to write as usual.

Pound scribbled frequent letters to me in pencil on cheap ruled paper. Some of the letters, especially the early ones, were desperate and frightening in tone; others were quite rational and matter of fact, having to do with personal and business affairs. Facsimiles of a number of these letters are reproduced here, with explanatory notes.

Pound customarily addressed me by my initials, J. C. This letter, like the others, was written from St. Elizabeths Hospital, which is abbreviated, "S. Liz." The word "mute" I believe refers to my advice to Pound to stand mute at the time of arraignment. Olson was a doctor who apparently gave him some comfort. The word "transfer" I believe means transfer from Gallinger Hospital to St. Elizabeths Hospital.

Wednes. night

S Liz

J C

Problem now is
not to go stark
screaming hysteric
cent CENT pure cent 24
hours per day
relapse after comfort of
Tuesday = I mute.
MUTE

Olson saved my life.

Young doctors absolutely
useless -

must have 15
minutes same
conversation daily

Young

Transfer

velocity after
stupor
Tremendous

enormous work
to be
done.

+ no driving
force

+ everyone's
incapacitude

very
fatiguing

This letter was written from the prison ward at St. Elizabeths, the "Dungeon," on a Sunday, *"Domenica,"* at the end of January, 1946. The salutation at the end *"aiuto"* is the Italian word for help.

end of Dungeon
6 Jan, Domenica

mental Torture
constitution a religion
a world lost
grey mist barrier impossible
ignorance absolute
anonyme
futility of 'might have been
coherent areas
constantly
invaded
a
into
Pound

In January, 1946, a few days before this letter was written, I had told Pound that there would be a jury trial a few weeks later at which psychiatrists would testify as to his fitness to be tried for treason. Pound was concerned about accusations of anti-Semitism. Here he tries to explain his position. Note the reference at the foot of this letter to the Constitution, which Pound felt he had been trying to protect from the machinations of usurers.

J. Cornell . atty.

S. Liz
22 Jan

As no one ever listens
To end of sentence or paragraf.
you might note that am
Zionist (@ least to xtent
of having Zionist plan - (no longer
much of life they wd ever
use it) - at least worked out
plan. to financing —
+ a SOLUTION. not conscripting
Einstein + non-zionists.

= memory of
Andre Spire
+ others.

E Pound

For the constitution -
remember that

= programme 3+1 points
+ also go finance . + sound basis.

Pound was fond of puns, of which there are several in this letter. He had asked me to subscribe in his name to *Newsweek* magazine, which he calls "snoozeweek." He complains that the magazine had not yet arrived.

S. Lit 21 F.

What we want now is papers as efficient as Time - Slit Digest & snooze week. That will occasionally print the Truth

gt D shit has been the "Hold down" on all real foreign news since 1927. (AT LEAST)

=

News Week has never Gone. YET. =

Has any real news re Luciano the lucky pimp ?

If I had address of some Bloomsbuggy lit. mag. I might trace a few human reliques.

Yrs EP

r. Woodward

This letter was written from St. Elizabeths March 12, 1946. It refers to a power of attorney which I had asked Dr. Overholser to permit Pound to execute on the ground that he had sufficient understanding of his publishing affairs to authorize me to collect his royalties for him and have other dealings with publishers. "D. P." refers to Pound's wife Dorothy.

S. L 1 2 12
M.

Dear J.C.

Would it be suitable
to say. Pow. of Atty. in
all matters pertaining to
publishing, collecting money
due me, & ordinary
routine,
connected therewith

ordinary
routine
perhaps
too general
a term
??

yes. the Personae is
for Jas.

If D.P. arrives she might
attend to various things.
IF, large if = she gets
the transport she is looking for.

E Pound

This letter was written from St. Elizabeths March 24, 1946. The Italian word for March is *Marzo* which Pound abbreviates "Mz." "Jas" refers to James Laughlin, Pound's American publisher. "Faber" refers to Faber & Faber, London publishers with whom T. S. Eliot was associated. The signature appears to be a profile of a face and is not Pound's usual signature.

Dr J.L. 20 Mz.

S Eliz.

Will send the pow. of atty as soon as get notary.

Next point is to get Jas. to understand need of putting a nucleus of civilization — more organic than a "Five foot shelf" + to tootle the suiter.

=

I don't suppose Faber moves is less than a geolog. epoch. or that you can usefully build fire under Eliot > or that there is any news get from that 1/4 er.

E. Pound

8 Ap. since heard from Eliot.

This letter was written April 16, 1946 from St. Elizabeths. "Moore" is Arthur V. Moore, London solicitor of the firm of Shakespear & Parkyn. "Pollinger" and "Curtis Brown" are London literary agents from whom royalties may have been due Pound.

(S. El. feb 28. 14 — 46

Dear J C

As you've that pow. of atty please air-mail to Moore TO collect what he can from Pollinger; & from Curtis Brown & hold it; NOT send anything here. ‖

= (Eliot knows where Faber paid)

Also in minor way cd/ you see that my deposit here is so fixed that small supply orders (for 20 cents worth of saltine biscuit etc.) don't get held up 3 weeks.

E Pound

James Laughlin, referred to as "Jas," was fond of skiing and frequently absent from his office for such purpose. The postscript on the back of this letter refers to a request Pound had made that I arrange for books and papers which he had left at Gallinger Hospital to be sent over to St. Elizabeths. In response to his request for novels, I sent him a dozen or so from a second-hand book store.

D [illegible] E   S. Eliz. 36
  [illegible]

"America" If a weekly called
(Catholic ? advance)
still exists. I shd. like 6 months
sub.

Don't know that News Week
is worth renewal.

IF you can pay $10. to
Mrs V. B. Jordan
195 Jefferson Ave
~~Tenaffly~~ Tenafly
Tenafly N.J.

she. cd/ attend to
future trifles of this sort
& save yr. office Time

Does anyone attend to
Jas' business when he is
ski-ing ?.

E Pound

vide
verso

Papers,
letters, &
books, had
@ gallinger, not
yet delivered to
me.

---

anybody who wants,
to send me
novels, not criticism
or high brow trash
can do so
— welcome

The letter on the next two pages was written May 4, 1946 about fees to be charged for inclusion of Pound's poems in anthologies, with a postscript about unanswered letters which Pound had left at Gallinger Hospital.

S Ezra

4 May

Dear J.C.

$25 per poem has been the minimum anthology fee for years & years

with $50 for a canto

(Has regular)

a part ça no comment

except that so far as I recollect I was never taken to Milan.

= I don't suggest litigation — but information

point academic.

the rate of anth fee is for yr future guidance. as well as historic information —

Thanks for other information etc.

EP

V. the P.S.

P.S. 3

There were several letters & the
galleys papers that I was
too ~~___~~ exhausted to
answer @ that time
& I have (not the letters)
but names & addresses of
people not members of family
or regular correspondents
—
There were several books
some with annotations

Have you read
"A Bell for
Adano"
by J Hersey
?

This letter is dated "3, *Lug.*," the Italian word for July being *Luglio.* Kirby was a poet who had sent me some verses to be forwarded to Pound. Pound's letterhead *"J'ayme donc je suis"* is a paraphrase of Descartes' famous aphorism *"Je pense donc je suis."*

3. Aug
later
S. Liz.

ezra pound

J'AYME DONC JE SUIS

Dear JG

yrs. 2nd inst just come.

Damn all Kirby is a good poet as well why aint I heard of him sooner.

sound verse is rare.

Also gt nooz in today's wypers.

fr to note - contents of yrn new but now noted

EP

This letter was written January 19, 1947 from St. Elizabeths in response to my inquiry about allowing an anthologist to use some of Pound's poems without paying for them.

S. Liz

J'AYME DONC JE SUIS

19 June

ezra pound

D. J. =

Ask the buggah
what his salary is,
+
why he shouldn't pay
for a round
of drinks

S.V.P.
+ will ~~also~~

E P

Thanks.
+ sorry you
shd. be bothered.

This letter refers to a book review in the New York *Herald Tribune* which mentioned Pound's alleged crime in a way which he felt inconsistent with his plea of not guilty.

ezra pound

J'AYME DONC JE SUIS

17 July

1 L—

Dear J.C.

Considering what you have told me is it not the N.Y. Herald-Trib Weekly Bk. Rev

p. 17 July 14 — Reprints new Editions etc.

a definite libel

of exactly the kind one wd/ expect from pseudonymous coward in this particular filthy entourage = ? Typical reviewer & book chatter

E

Not to be confused with Patterson's chicken shit in the woman's Turn.

At any rate you told me I pled not-guilty i.e. my plea equivalent.

Pound felt that he was an expert on European affairs and that the United States government was bungling in Greece and Yugoslavia, relying upon advice no more reliable than that of friends of the notorious Lucky Luciano, who had been deported from the United States to Italy.

Have the — — — d—n fools made enough mess in greece. Jugslavia etc to realize YET

that they need something more reliable than Lucky Luciano's friends in Italy,

in fact need help of ANYone who knows a b—dy thing about Europe. n the mediterranean.

For an account of the dispute with Bennett Cerf about his column in *The Saturday Review of Literature,* see pages 112-115.

S Eliz.

Not (1) me holding up answer to yr. last was ready to answer
the day it came. (as per. enc).

(2)
Wd any interest attatch # to fact that Cerf has in his carefully selected [belated, reed here]
mind [not to think of what he did not print] printed letter containing
falsehood (defamatory) that can be proved to be false
without needing any statement from me to that effect?).

E Pound

apart from indicating mentality of Sat. Rev. & the people who regard Cerf as a comic q. affeal.

Pound found the slurs upon him which had been printed in various newspapers and magazines more objectionable than the remarks of Bennett Cerf in *The Saturday Review of Literature*.

I don't weep over mere nastiness , but object to libel .
Present dirt tries to overlook Guarantee fromItal. govt
that I wd/ not be asked to (and never was asked to)
say anything vs/ conscience or duties as Am. Cit.

Dear Mr. Cornell. Thanks for copy of your
letter to Sat. Rev. of Lit.
EP. is not interested in the question of his
sanity - but in establishing that he did
NOT commit treason - The treason was in
the White House, not in Rapallo -- & people
are beginning to see that at last.

Sincerely
Dorothy Pound.

This was written in January, 1948. Pound did not understand why his bank accounts were being blocked by the Alien Property Custodian under a law directed at nationals of Italy and other enemy countries.

Dea J.C.
are yYOU stark raving. ??

When the hell and WHO proclaimed me a italian national.

NO such notice ever served onme. Apart from Roosevelt being supreme swine and be trayer and all the state d4pt/ tained with moral leprosy from him.

IF I were italian , how the heel do they xharge me as an american ?

"eally LUNACY is abroad worsre than in S.Liz.

and by what LAW . not that there is any inthe U.S. / do the under clerks PROCLAIM the citizen this ort that.

The following three page letter was typewritten for her husband by Dorothy Pound on October 26, 1948. The longhand insertion on the first page was added by Ezra Pound.

J.C. has neve r bothered to find out what EP's positionwas .

BUT this libe l consists in lying assumption that EP. accepted what the smear labled Fascism / whereas E.P. took specific stands

and Jefferson was finally quoted on fascist posters.

One does NOT expect much of the S,Rev. Lit / But certain lies shd/ be challenged.

The o ld bitch inthe W,H, was provided with a copy of Jeff/Muss wherein certain definitions ar e made. Naturally there is nolaw in the u.s. and the press is mainly still under Roosevelt's rump

.I take it the law about cases sub judice has passed into kinnocuous dessuetude ,And that etc.

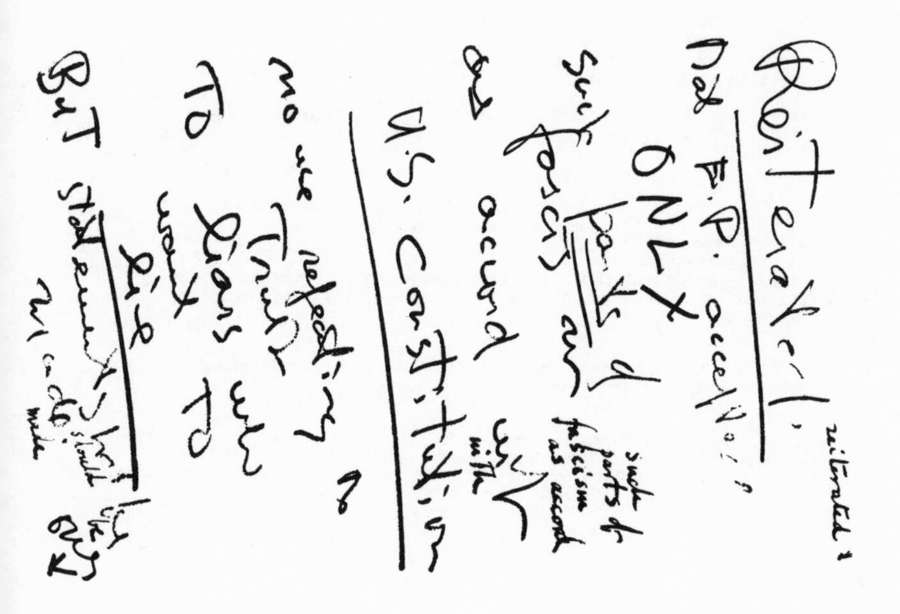

But if any interest in Constitution and legality still exists . might be almost time to list violations of law , let alone decency committed by the Morgenthau treasury plus satilites and affinities in case of said E.H P.

as to a short time at Pisa , confessedly " easier to hold you under military law , becausse considered guilty until proved innocent. "

Statement in Merlo Giallo just rcd/ by R.M. degli Uberti son of Admiral degli Uberti , head of Italian naval press bureau , AND the admiral knew , and the Uberti's since Farinata saved Florence from being destroyed in a pre-Dantesca civil war , do not lie.

any how on Sept 7th. a letter protesting against listing E.P. with Amery , Sforza and others.

" Ma Ezra Pound non era

E.P was not a propagandist in the pay of a foreign government, He has not betrayed America but tried to prevent America from betraying Mother Europe.

...

From 1935 he extended his fight against the reign of usury and speculation - the usurocracy -

(parenthesis you cant mention this in the Baruch Morgenthau press " free press " as Jackson wd/ call it)

but still if it dont get beyond the walls of the office you can read it.

to those international manifestations of its power which , via the crazy politics of Roosevelt might lead to the collapse of European civilization.

This battle he conducted alone , without help , understood perhaps only by his enemies.

...

Even during the microphone war and in the Axis press , maintaining ever his own independence he fought what was his personal battle to make America understand the folly she was committing. Not a traitor , Mr Editor , a prophet. "

after WHKH which , with a burst of italian
idolatry for anything U.S.A. he goes on to say that
the Americans have understood this.

I think they will in another 80 years. But to say
that they have leads me to think the European perspective
is not yet exact.

" And the mud stays MUD " and Guinicelli has rema ked.

Never mind state of mind / No emphasis has been placed on
Ital govt. promise that shd/ not be asked to say anythung
vs/ conscience and duty.

After 12 years of frankie the perjurer
who had sworn to support the const / etc.

the am/ people is too degraded to understand that I was
dealing with men of honour (phrase as alien to U,S. as if it
had been last used inthe Morte d'Arthur)

and that the
promise was kept by them , as it wd/ not have been by Roosevelt or
or any of the men about him.

However , that also will come out
some day.

Also where does Norman get that trype about friends' doors closed.

I spent only one night in a hotel all the time I was
here , and I came unexpected / that one night was
getting into N.Y. late and wanting to be there in the a.m.

I hear however that some of the enemy are feeling depressed.

and
so
on

if C/ hasnt a list of the illegalities. durations etc.
one might supply him.

Greetings
Dorothy Pound.

The most faithful and concerned of Pound's friends was T. S. Eliot. Each year Eliot visited the United States to give lectures and on business, never failing to call upon me to inquire about Pound and offer advice and assistance. These meetings took place at my office, at the office of Eliot's New York publishers, or at luncheon in a Greenwich Village restaurant and on one occasion at the Century Club, where we were joined by Horace Gregory, Allen Tate, James Laughlin and other literary figures.

I was much taken with Eliot. Born in St. Louis, he had settled in London and had become a British subject. After living for many years in England, he acquired, along with his British citizenship, a British accent, Savile Row tailoring and an umbrella. Tall, stoop-shouldered, peering over his spectacles and speaking in careful, clipped tones, Eliot was the impersonation of "Old Possum".

Pound and Eliot had long been intimate friends. It was Pound who was credited by Eliot with having, by his criticism and cutting, made Eliot's *Waste Land* a landmark in modern poetry. The generosity which Pound had always shown toward his literary friends was now repaid. Throughout Pound's incarceration, Eliot was his faithful friend, his refuge and his strength.

After a visit to Pound at the hospital, Eliot wrote me:

LETTER FROM T. S. ELIOT TO JULIEN CORNELL

November 24, 1948

My dear Cornell,

After my visit to St. Elizabeth's Hospital I came away with one very clear notion of something that should be done for Ezra Pound which his well-being seems to me to require.

Mrs. Pound told me that Pound was only allowed out of doors at the times when the other inmates of his ward were allowed to go out, under the supervision of a warder. It seems to me that it ought to be permissible for him to go out alone in the grounds with his wife, and with her responsible for his returning in due time. This would, incidentally, give a relatively greater degree of privacy than is possible under the conditions in which he can be visited indoors. I am not in the least suggesting that he should be allowed to leave the grounds.

Could you take this point up with Dr. Overholser? I saw him only before I had visited Pound, and before Mrs. Pound had told me of this restriction. Surely he is entitled to have some fresh air daily, upon this condition.

I also think that it would be desirable to enquire whether there is not some other building on the grounds in which he could be confined, where he could have somewhat more normal conditions, and not be among patients of the types of insanity among which he is at present.

I am writing in some haste, as I have still to pack for my departure from Princeton tomorrow.

Yours sincerely

T. S. ELIOT

I sent a copy of the foregoing letter to Dr. Overholser, who replied:

LETTER FROM DR. OVERHOLSER TO JULIEN CORNELL

I have your letter of November 29th enclosing the inquiry from Mr. T. S. Eliot about Mr. Ezra Pound. I had a brief talk with Mr. Eliot at the time of his visit to Washington, but unfortunately as he says in his letter, this was before he had seen Mr. Pound. I have some hesitation in accepting the suggestions made by Mr. Eliot. It remains a fact that Mr. Pound is under indictment for the most serious crime in the calendar and that he has at the present time far more privileges than any other prisoner in the Hospital. He is on a quiet ward, has a room by himself and is allowed a good deal of latitude in the way he occupies himself. His wife visits him very frequently. When I found that the walking parties had been suspended in the winter I saw to it that on days when the weather was good these were reinstituted, but I found that Mr. Pound refused to go on any but the first.

He has supreme contempt for the patients on the ward regardless of the ward he might be on since he is inclined to be rather supercilious in his views of practically everyone with whom he comes in contact.

I can assure you that we shall do everything within reason for the comfort of Mr. Pound, but in spite of his being a well known author, I question whether I should put myself in the position of giving unusual privileges to him over and above those which he already enjoys.

Yours very truly,

WINFRED OVERHOLSER

Being allowed to have any visitors he chose and being a most gregarious person, Pound was sought out by many cranks and publicity seekers who used him for their own purposes. Those who sought publicity at Pound's expense included John Kasper, the notorious racist, and Eustace Mullins, who wrote a very egotistical book about Pound.

There were two controversies in the newspapers during this period which call for comment.

The first of these arose when the publisher Bennett Cerf was preparing a Modern Library edition of Conrad Aiken's anthology of poetry. Aiken had included in the earlier edition twelve poems by Ezra Pound, but Cerf refused now to print anything by Pound on the ground that he was a fascist and a traitor. Aiken insisted that if Pound's poems were excluded from the anthology, Cerf would have to print an explanatory note to the effect that Aiken had selected these twelve poems but the publisher had refused to print them. This episode is told in a news items, Cerf's column in *The Saturday Review of Literature* and my correspondence with him, which follow:

NEW YORK TIMES, MARCH 14, 1946

Yielding to critics who protested the exclusion from a poetry anthology of twelve poems by Ezra Pound, accused of nineteen acts of treason, Bennett Cerf, president of Random House, yesterday called the exclusion "an error in judgment" and announced his decision to include the poems in future editions of the volume. The publisher said that by his reversal he hoped to "remove any possible hint of suppression." * * *

The controversy started with the appearance several months ago of a new volume in the Modern Library, issued by Random House, entitled "An Anthology of Famous English and American Poetry." When Conrad Aiken, editor of the American section, included twelve poems by Pound Mr. Cerf ruled them out of the volume on the grounds that a publisher has the privilege of refusing to issue under his imprint the works of proclaimed Fascists. Mr. Aiken, also a poet, agreed to the omission provided the volume would list the titles he had intended to include as well as the publisher's note explaining that the editor had been overruled.

"We exceeded our prerogative," Mr. Cerf will say in a forthcoming issue of The Saturday Review of Literature, in which he conducts a regular column. * * *

Mr. Cerf said yesterday that while he had changed his mind he was "an angry convert." * * *

LETTER FROM JULIEN CORNELL TO BENNETT CERF

March 15, 1946

Dear Sir:

As attorney for Ezra Pound I wish to inform you that you may not publish his poems in your Modern Library anthology until you have received authority to do so. Mr. Pound has not given his permission, and any ostensible authority which you may have obtained from Liveright Publishing Corporation as publishers of Pound's collected poems is invalid because their contract with him expired on April 12, 1944, after which date they had no power to give such authority.

A request for permission to include Mr. Pound's poems in your anthology will not be considered unless you agree to refrain from printing in connection therewith any derogatory statements concerning him such as your proposed statement that he is "a contemptible betrayer of his country."

I regard this statement as libellous. Mr. Pound has not been proved guilty, and if he is brought to trial I believe that he will be acquitted on the ground that he has been insane for many years.

In any case, it must be presumed, under the laws of a democratic country and the rules of fair play, that he is innocent until proved guilty. I would suggest that you print a retraction and apology in the next issue of the Saturday Review of Literature, in which your statement appeared.

Sincerely yours,

JULIEN CORNELL

SATURDAY REVIEW OF LITERATURE, MARCH 16, 1946; EXCERPT FROM COLUMN "TRADE WINDS"

Readers' reactions to the Ezra Pound controversy, outlined in this column on February 9, are so evenly divided that I found it hard myself to believe the result. As of February 25, I had received 289 expressions of opinion; 142 opposed the exclusion of Pound poems from Conrad Aiken's new anthology of American poetry; 140 approved their exclusion. * * *

It is damn unpleasant to admit a mistake publicly, but I see no way out of it. I am thoroughly convinced that our omission of the Pound poems from the volume in question was an error in judgment, to be rectified as soon as possible. This does not mean that my abhorrence for Ezra Pound the man has abated one iota, or that the legal mumbo-jumbo declaring him "insane" is any more palatable to me. I base my conclusions on the following premises, emphasized so ably by many correspondents:

1. This was not a whole book by Pound; it was an anthology. We entrusted Conrad Aiken with the task. When he insisted on including Pound, we had the right to protest, or to refuse to publish the book altogether; we exceeded our prerogative in overriding him.

2. The poems themselves contained nothing pernicious. Many correspondents questioned Pound's right as a poet to be included in a representative anthology of American verse, but I need scarcely point out that this had absolutely nothing to do with the issue involved.

3. Many of the letters upholding my original stand, while deeply sincere, obviously sacrificed all logic for hot indignation. This, of course, is precisely the accusation made against me by Lewis

Gannett. The growing suspicion that he might be right was deeply disturbing.

4. The clinching argument was: "Once begun, where can you draw the line in this sort of thing?" If Pound is thrown out of a Modern Library anthology, have not other readers the right to demand the elimination of Nietzsche, or Marx's "Capital," or Hamsun's "Growth of the Soil"? This leads straight to the sort of censorship, and assumption of the right to tell others what they should and should not read, that I have fought against for years. * * *

BENNETT CERF

LETTER FROM JULIEN CORNELL TO BENNETT CERF

May 10, 1946

Dear Mr. Cerf:

This is to let you know that I have received from Ezra Pound approval for publication by Random House in the Modern Library anthology of the 12 poems selected by Mr. Aiken, on the condition that nothing concerning Mr. Pound will be printed in the anthology except the following explanatory note, the text of which was suggested by you:

> "After the publishers of the Modern Library omitted the poems of Ezra Pound from the first edition of this volume, a veritable avalanche of praise and blame, equally divided, descended upon them.
>
> Nothing could have been farther from the intention of the publishers than to exercise arbitrary rights of censorship. We now have decided to include these poems of Ezra Pound in order to remove any possible hint of suppression, and because we concede that it may be wrong to confuse Pound the poet with Pound the man."

Mr. Pound has agreed to accept $300 in payment for the poems.

Sincerely yours,

JULIEN CORNELL

There was another controversy about Pound which stirred up tremendous excitement when he was awarded the Bollingen Prize by the Library of Congress.

The Bollingen Foundation had been established by Paul Mellon, a son of Andrew Mellon, former Secretary of the Treasury. The Foundation had made a grant to the Library of Congress which was to award an annual prize of $1,000 for the best volume of poetry published in the preceding year. The award was to be made by a jury drawn from the Fellows in American Letters of the Library of Congress. Although Pound was still under indictment for treason, nevertheless, the Library of Congress awarded him the Bollingen Prize.

The spectacle of a government institution awarding a prize to a man whom the same government had indicted for treason was a source of acute irritation to some people and rich amusement to others.

The prize was not awarded without thought having been given to the objections which might arise. I was working in Paris when I received the following letter from Leonie Adams, Consultant in Poetry of the Library of Congress, telling me that the committee in charge of the Bollingen award had recommended that it be given to Ezra Pound provided that no difficulties would be caused either to him or to the Library.

LETTER FROM LEONIE ADAMS TO JULIEN CORNELL

Dear Mr. Cornell:

I write you at the suggestion of Mr. Robert Lowell, as chairman of the committee for awarding the Bollingen Prize of the Fellows in American Letters of the Library of Congress.

As you know it was voted at the Fellows' meeting to recommend Mr. Pound for this award, provided the special circumstances do not make this too difficult for the Library or Mr. Pound.

Recently information has come to me from those investigating the matter from the Library's standpoint that there is now some question of reviewing Mr. Pound's case in order to determine on a legal finding of insanity, and in general it is their opinion that publicity at this time would be most unfortunate. This opinion has also been expressed by someone in a position to know a good deal unofficially about Department of Justice attitudes.

The Committee would be very grateful for some word from you before reporting to the Fellows who are to be asked to ratify the vote.

Very sincerely yours,

LEONIE ADAMS
Poetry Chair

Leonie Adams, in addition to being the Poetry Consultant, was also Chairman for the year 1949 of the Fellows in American Letters of the Library of Congress. Under the terms of the Bollingen Prize award, the Fellows were the jury which would make the award.

Although the Bollingen Prize was awarded by the Library of Congress, the staff of the Library had no part in the selection of Ezra Pound as the recipient of the award, leaving the matter entirely in the hands of the jury.

This led to the paradoxical result that a man who was under a treason indictment obtained by the Department of Justice received a prize from another branch of the Government.

The effect of the award on Ezra Pound personally was discussed in my reply to Leonie Adams' letter:

LETTER FROM JULIEN CORNELL TO LEONIE ADAMS

February 7, 1949

Dear Leonie Adams:

This is in reply to your letter about the Bollingen prize, which reaches me in Paris—hence the delay in getting this answer to you.

I understand that the Fellows in American Letters of the Library of Congress have recommended that the prize be awarded to Ezra Pound provided that there are no obstacles presented by the circumstances in which Mr. Pound finds himself, either for the Library or Mr. Pound.

I assume that you are familiar with the legal proceedings previously had, which resulted in a decision by the United States District Court for the District of Columbia that Mr. Pound is of unsound mind and by reason thereof is unable to stand trial for treason. The indictment is still pending, but in my opinion will never be tried, as the doctors believe there will be no recovery sufficient to enable Mr. Pound to stand trial.

You should also understand that Mr. Pound is at present confined in St. Elizabeths Hospital, a U. S. government institution, under an order of the same court, for an indefinite period, and that Dorothy Pound, his wife, was appointed by the court as Committee of his property. (The prize, if awarded, should be given to her as his legal representative.)

At one time, Mrs. Pound contemplated a habeas corpus proceeding seeking the release of her husband on the ground that he cannot be restored to sanity, hence can never be tried for treason, yet is presumed to be innocent and is not in need of close confinement, which is tantamount to imprisonment of an innocent man. The question of law presented here is a novel one, and the case also being one in which the public exhibited much interest, such a proceeding would probably have to be appealed through the United States Supreme Court. The decision would depend however, on questions of constitutional law, and would not, I think, be affected substantially by public opinion regarding Mr. Pound personally, or his literary or political position. Furthermore, the habeas corpus proceeding has been abandoned upon instructions of Mrs. Pound. Therefore, I do not believe that Mr. Pound's legal position would be in any way affected by the awarding of the prize.

As for Mr. Pound's personal welfare, apart from legal considerations, I should tell you that there appears to be no prospect for his release from the hospital. I have taken up this question with Dr. Winfred Overholser, Superintendent of St. Elizabeths, and he feels unable to release Mr. Pound except in case of recovery, when Mr. Pound would be returned to the court. Unquestionably, the hospital authorities are bound by court order to keep Mr. Pound in custody, but they have, as you may know, done a great deal to give him special privileges pertinent to his need for intellectual and cultural activity. Not only must Mr. Pound be held in custody, but also he cannot be given any greater freedom than he now has, within the institution. Here again, therefore, the public interest which would be prompted by the award of the prize would have no effect, in my judgment, on his position. I must hasten to add that this view is based largely on the dispassionate and firm qualities which I have found in Dr. Overholser. I am sure that he would not be affected by public opinion, either from the press or the Fellows of the Library of Congress, in his treatment of his patient and his performance of his public duty under the law.

As regards Mr. Pound's welfare, my conclusion is that the awarding of the Bollingen Prize to him would in no respect jeopardize his legal or personal position, but on the contrary, such recognition would be welcomed by him, and might serve to support his wavering ego. You can judge as well as I what effect the award might have on Mr. Pound's psyche, but I feel sure it could do no harm and might do much good. Those who are imprisoned always feel forgotten and isolated, and appreciate deeply their contacts with the outside world.

From the foregoing, I hope that you may be able to decide whether the awarding of the prize would present any difficulties to the Library of Congress. If you need further information in order to reach a decision, you may write me at my Paris office.

Sincerely yours,

JULIEN CORNELL

NEW YORK HERALD TRIBUNE, FEBRUARY 21, 1949

Washington, February 20, 1949.—Ezra Pound, the sixty-three-year-old eccentric poet who escaped trial for treason three years ago when he was committed to a mental institution, won the $1,000 Bollingen Prize yesterday for the best poetry published in 1948.

The selection was made by a jury of Fellows in American Letters of the Library of Congress. The jurors were T. S. Eliot, Paul Green, Robert Lowell, Katherine Ann Porter, Karl Shapiro, Allen Tate, Willard Thorp, Robert Penn Warren, Conrad Aiken, Louise Bogan, W. H. Auden, Katherine Garrison Chapin, Leonie Adams and the late Theodore Spencer.

The award was made for Pound's "Pisan Cantos," published last year as a "New Directions" book by James Laughlin. The book consists of the last ten of the eighty-four cantos which Pound has published against his promise to write 100. * * *

Pound's work, the jurors held, "represents the highest achievement of American poetry in the year for which the award is made." The jurors, however, explained their decision to recognize Pound's work despite objections which might be raised against him politically.

"The Fellows are aware," the jurors said, "that objections may be made to awarding a prize to a man situated as is Mr. Pound. In their view, however, the possibility of such objection did not alter the responsibility assumed by the jury of selection. This was to make a choice for the award among the eligible books, provided any one merited such recognition, according to the stated terms of the Bollingen Prize. To permit other considerations than that of poetic achievement to sway the decision would destroy the significance of the award and would in principle deny the validity of that objective perception of value on which any civilized society must rest."

This was the first award of what is to be an annual selection. The prize, according to the Library of Congress, which made yesterday's announcement, was established a year ago and was made possible by a gift of money from the Bollingen Foundation, New York.

The Bollingen Foundation was established some time ago by the family of the late Andrew W. Mellon, Secretary of the Treasury in the Administrations of Presidents Harding, Coolidge and Hoover and later Ambassador to the Court of St. James.

VIII

RETURN TO ITALY

EZRA POUND REMAINED at St. Elizabeths Hospital until April 1958, more than twelve years in the hospital and thirteen years in confinement altogether from the time when he was arrested in Italy.

As time went on, the hue and cry for vengeance against Pound and others accused of crimes arising out of the war faded away. The good will and generosity which are characteristic of the American people created a ground swell of sympathy for him. There was increasing criticism of the government for keeping him incarcerated. Even *Life* magazine, ultra-conservative in its politics, came out with a strong plea for Pound's release in the following editorial:

EDITORIAL FROM "LIFE," FEBRUARY 6, 1956

An Artist Confined

Tokyo Rose got out of jail the other day. This American citizen, who did her considerable best to undermine American morale during World War II, has now finished her sentence as a war criminal. The Nazi storm trooper responsible for the Malmedy massacre of 1944, General Dietrich, is also out of jail, one of a growing line of commutees and parolees.

If their crimes can be atoned or forgotten in 10 years, attention is surely due the case of Ezra Pound, who has been incarcerated for the same length of time. His prison is St. Elizabeths in Washington, the federal hospital for the insane. He is confined, with the consent of his lawyer, to avoid a treason trial for which he is mentally unfit. He is fit to work on his Chinese translations (he is one of the best translators of poetry who ever lived), to receive friends and disciples, and to reiterate the political and economic nonsense (a weird and ineffective mixture of social credit and anti-Semitism) which he broadcast for Mussolini during the war. Pound's indictment has no statute of limitations. It will never be tried (and Pound will therefore never be eligible for pardon) as long as he stays in St. Elizabeths. There he sits, busy and batty, free alike of self-pity and remorse.

In France and Italy, where Pound lived for years, the press frequently erupts with appeals to the U. S. government to release and forgive a distinguished old man. They frequently misrepresent the case, which is technically complicated, but they are right that our government has it in its power to quash his indictment. Thereafter his insanity might be redefined (it is not dangerous) so that he could return to Europe if he wants. One Italian deputy made a telling point: "After all, if the U. S. can send us back such characters as Luciano without our asking for them, can't the U. S. also send us Ezra Pound upon our request?"

Seven years ago, before war passions had cooled, Pound was given the Bollingen poetry award. It stirred up a fuss from Congress to Bohemia. Literary men cudgeled such eternal questions as whether poets should be judged by their politics. It would be no service to Pound, or to America, to revive these arguments. If his case is to be reconsidered at all, it should be without hatred or pity, and in the light of justice in comparable cases. These range from turncoats Best and Chandler, who got life, to the repentant P. G. Wodehouse, who was not even indicted.

Our European critics use the Pound case to argue that American civilization is indifferent to its own poets and artists, or has ears only for their praise. Pound turned his back on America in 1907. He led a generation of expatriates and experimenters which, as he once confessed, "was unable to work out a code for action"; in his case fascism filled this gap. As Mark Van Doren put it, Pound "ran out of bounds in his pursuit of a society where artists might live." But meanwhile he has done more to serve the art of English poetry, to keep its practice alive and its standards high, than any living man.

Pound's room at St. Elizabeths has been called "a closet which contains a national skeleton." There may be good arguments for keeping him there, but there are none for pretending he doesn't exist. The crimes of World War II have aged to the point of requital, parole or forgiveness. For this reason, if no other, the arguments for quashing the indictment against Ezra Pound should be publicly considered.

Ezra Pound was sixty years old when he was brought to Washington for trial. He had now reached the age of seventy-two, after twelve years in St. Elizabeths Hospital. It appeared probable that he would die there, despite the fact that he was still presumed innocent in the eyes of the law and there was also considerable doubt if he was sane enough to have been responsible for the opinions which he had expressed from Rome. Then too, there was the question whether the broadcasts were treasonable. Now that the war was long over, much of what Pound had been saying appeared to have been permissible criticism of his government.

On all these counts, there was no longer any desire on the part of the United States Government to punish Pound, but on the other hand it was not easy, once having prosecuted him, to let him go gracefully.

Pound's liberation was accomplished almost single-handedly by one man, the New England poet Robert Frost, a universally admired, unofficial "poet laureate", who was later invited by President Kennedy to compose and recite a poem at his inaugural.

Frost made it his business to free Pound. He went to his friend Sherman Adams, also from New England, who was assistant to President Eisenhower, and had more power in the government than anyone but the President himself. Frost enlisted the sympathy and aid of Adams in having Pound released. Adams took the matter up with the Department of Justice, which ordered an investigation by the Federal Bureau of Investigation.

These negotiations were, of course, carried on in private. The first I knew about the matter was when two FBI agents came to my office and questioned me for an hour or more about the Pound case. Before answering any questions I wanted to know why they were making an investigation. They told me that the Attorney General was considering the possibility of releasing Pound. I told them that I had not seen Pound for several years but so far as I knew there was no other attorney acting for him.

The FBI men wanted to know in particular why the Department of Justice, at the time of Pound's sanity hearing, had not put up a better fight. I explained to them that in view of the unanimous opinion of the government's own doctors, there was nothing which any lawyer could do except to make sure the matter had a full hearing. Matlack's case was hopeless and he knew it. I also told the FBI agents that in my opinion the situation never would have arisen if the army psychiatrists at the Pisa concentration camp had not blundered in their failure to diagnose Pound's illness. The agents asked: "Was he really insane; was he really unfit to be tried and why was he any different from the other war criminals?" The answer, of course, may be found in the testimony of the four psychiatrists, all of them most eminent in their profession, men of sound judgment who expressed not the slightest doubt as to Pound's condition.

Many years earlier I had arranged for the appointment of Mrs. Pound as "committee" of the person and property of her husband by the District of Columbia Court in order that she might handle his business affairs. She would, therefore, have to initiate any legal proceedings for his release. There were three possibilities: (1) a habeas corpus proceeding to test the legality of his confinement; this had already been tried in the District Court but never tested in the higher courts; (2) a request for a Presidential pardon, but this did not seem appropriate because Pound had never been convicted of anything and in any case, he would not ask for a pardon because this would have been an admission of guilt, which he had always strenuously denied; (3) a motion to dismiss the indictment on the ground that there was no possibility of his ever being tried; this was a simple procedure and a court would probably grant the motion if the Department of Justice consented to it.

Without consulting Mrs. Pound, Frost went to Thurman Arnold, prominent Washington lawyer, head of the firm of Arnold, Fortas and Porter.

Arnold had been a professor at Yale Law School when I was there. Later he was in charge of the anti-trust division of the Department of Justice, then a judge of the United States Circuit Court of Appeals for the District of Columbia and after that he established one of the most successful law firms in the city of Washington. He was well-known for his legal acumen, upright character and forceful personality. Arnold told Frost that he would be willing to take the case.

Of course, Mrs. Pound would have to employ Arnold and under the ethics of the legal profession, he could not suggest this to her but the initiative would have to come from Frost. Arnold was placed in a very embarrassing position because Frost that very day released to the newspapers a statement that Arnold was going to represent Pound in a motion for the dismissal of the indictment. The first Mrs. Pound knew of the matter was when she read in the newspapers that Arnold had become her attorney. The following day, Mrs. Pound came to Arnold's office and readily agreed to the arrangement which Frost had made.

Motion papers were prepared by Arnold supported by an affidavit of Dr. Overholser, a brief memorandum of law and a statement by Robert Frost to which he attached statements which he had obtained from a large number of other literary men urging Pound's release. These papers are printed here, together with an article from the *New York Times* describing the scene in the courtroom. The entire matter is recounted in Thurman Arnold's book *Fair Fights and Foul* at pp. 236-242.

MOTION IN UNITED STATES DISTRICT COURT FOR THE DISTRICT OF COLUMBIA TO DISMISS INDICTMENT, APRIL 1958

Comes now Ezra Pound, defendant, through his committee, Mrs. Dorothy Shakespear Pound, and moves that the indictment in the above-entitled proceeding be dismissed.

And for grounds of the said motion, he respectfully represents:

1. On November 26, 1945, defendant was indicted on charges of treason relating to certain radio broadcasts made by defendant in

Italy during World War II. On November 27, 1945, he stood mute on arraignment and a plea of not guilty to that indictment was entered by the Court. On December 4, 1945, defendant was admitted to Gallinger Hospital. On December 14, 1945, in pursuance of an appointment by this Court, Drs. Winfred Overholser, Marion R. King, Joseph L. Gilbert and Wendell Muncie submitted a joint written report to the Court that they had thoroughly examined the defendant on several occasions between December 4 and December 13, 1945, that it was their unanimous opinion that defendant was suffering from a paranoid state which rendered him mentally unfit to advise properly with counsel or to participate intelligently and reasonably in his own defense, and that he was insane and mentally unfit for trial. On January 18, 1946, the Court heard and granted a motion for a formal statutory inquisition to determine defendant's sanity. On February 13, 1946, the Court held such formal inquisition at which the jury, after hearing the evidence, report and conclusions of Drs. Overholser, King, Gilbert and Muncie, entered a formal verdict that the defendant was of unsound mind. Following the verdict, the defendant was committed to the custody of the United States and confined in Saint Elizabeths Hospital.

2. The defendant has remained in confinement at Saint Elizabeths Hospital since that time, where he has been the subject of constant and intense psychiatric tests, examinations, observation and study. As a result thereof, it is the opinion and conclusion of officials of Saint Elizabeths Hospital that defendant remains mentally unfit to advise properly with counsel or to participate intelligently and reasonably in his own defense and that he is insane and mentally unfit for trial, or to comprehend the nature of the charges against him.

3. Furthermore, it is the opinion and conclusion of these same officials that defendant's condition is permanent and incurable, that it cannot and will not respond to treatment and that trial on the charges against him will be forever impossible because of insanity.

4. Defendant is 72 years old. If the indictment against him is not dismissed he will die in Saint Elizabeths Hospital. He can never be brought to a state of mental competency or sanity sufficient

to advise properly with counsel, to participate intelligently and reasonably in his own defense or to comprehend the nature of the charges against him. There can be no benefit to the United States in maintaining him indefinitely in custody as a public charge because that custody cannot contribute to his recovery and defendant's release would not prejudice the interests of the United States. The inevitable effect of failure to dismiss the indictment will be life imprisonment on account of alleged acts and events which can never be put to proof.

5. The primary alleged acts and events on which the indictment is based occurred prior to July 25, 1943. In the ensuing fifteen years memories have faded and direct evidence by the constitutionally-established minimum of two witnesses to each of the various alleged acts and events have inevitably dissipated. In all probability, therefore, the United States lacks sufficient evidence to warrant a prosecution at this time.

6. Suitable arrangements for defendant's custody and care are otherwise available. In the event that the indictment is dismissed, Mrs. Dorothy Shakespear Pound, committee, proposes to apply for the delivery of the defendant from further confinement at Saint Elizabeths Hospital to her restraint and care with bond under such terms and conditions as will be appropriate to the public good and the best interests and peace of mind of the defendant in the remaining years of his life.

7. On the issues of fact thus presented, defendant respectfully requests a hearing.

WHEREFORE, Ezra Pound, defendant, by his committee, Mrs. Dorothy Shakespear Pound, respectfully moves that the indictment be dismissed.

Respectfully submitted,

THURMAN ARNOLD
WILLIAM D. ROGERS
ARNOLD, FORTAS & PORTER

AFFIDAVIT OF DR. WINFRED OVERHOLSER SWORN TO APRIL 14, 1958, IN SUPPORT OF MOTION TO DISMISS INDICTMENT

Dr. Winfred Overholser, being first duly sworn, deposes and says:

1. I am the Superintendent of Saint Elizabeths Hospital, Washington, District of Columbia.

2. Ezra Pound was admitted to Gallinger Hospital, Washington, District of Columbia, on December 4, 1945. Between that date and December 13, 1945, I and Drs. Joseph L. Gilbert, Marion R. King and Wendell Muncie each examined Ezra Pound on several occasions, separately and together, pursuant to appointment by the Honorable Bolitha J. Laws, Chief Justice, United States District Court. On December 14, 1945, I and Drs. Gilbert, King and Muncie submitted our joint report to the Chief Justice that Ezra Pound was suffering from a paranoid state which rendered him unfit to advise properly with counsel or to participate intelligently and reasonably in his own defense, and that he was insane and mentally unfit for trial on the criminal charges then pending against him. A copy of this joint report is attached hereto as Exhibit A.

3. On February 15, 1946, I testified to like effect at a formal inquisition as to sanity in respect to Ezra Pound.

4. Pursuant to the determination and verdict of the jury at the aforesaid inquisition, that Ezra Pound was of unsound mind, he was committed to Saint Elizabeths Hospital.

5. I have on a large number of occasions, both alone and with other psychiatrists of the staff of Saint Elizabeths Hospital and others, intensively tested, examined, observed and studied Ezra Pound.

6. If called to testify on a hearing in respect to dismissal of the pending criminal indictment against Ezra Pound, I will testify and state under oath that Ezra Pound is, and since December 4, 1945, has been, suffering from a paranoid state which has rendered and now renders him unfit to advise properly with counsel or to par-

ticipate intelligently and reasonably in his own defense, and that he was and is, and has continuously been, insane and mentally unfit for trial.

7. Furthermore, if called to testify on a hearing, I will testify and state under oath that the condition of Ezra Pound as thus described is permanent and incurable, that it will not and has not responded to treatment, that further professional therapeutic attention under hospital conditions would be of no avail and produce no beneficial results and that he is permanently and incurably insane.

8. Furthermore, if called to testify on a hearing, I will testify and state under oath that there is no likelihood, and indeed in my considered judgment and opinion no possibility, that the indictment pending against Ezra Pound can ever be tried because of the permanent and incurable condition of insanity of Ezra Pound, and that Ezra Pound will die insane in Saint Elizabeths Hospital without trial of the charges against him if the indictment remains pending.

9. Finally, if called to testify on a hearing, I will testify and state under oath that in my opinion, from examination of Ezra Pound made in 1945, within two to three years of the crimes charged in the indictment, there is a strong probability that the commission of the crime charged was the result of insanity, and I would therefore seriously doubt that prosecution could show criminal responsibility even if it were hypothetically assumed that Ezra Pound could regain sufficient sanity to be tried.

10. In the event that the indictment is dismissed, I will recommend the delivery of Ezra Pound from further confinement at Saint Elizabeths Hospital under suitable arrangements for his custody, care and restraint by his committee, Mrs. Dorothy Shakespear Pound. Further confinement can serve no therapeutic purpose. It would be a needless expense and burden upon the public facilities of the hospital. Ezra Pound is not a dangerous person and his release would not endanger the safety of other persons or the officers, the property, or other interests of the United States.

WINFRED OVERHOLSER

MEMORANDUM SUBMITTED IN SUPPORT OF MOTION TO DISMISS INDICTMENT, APRIL 1958

1. The motion to dismiss the indictment is properly addressed to the Court. The Court has inherent power to dismiss an indictment in circumstances where justice requires and where, as here, the United States will never be able to prosecute. *United States* v. *Pack,* 20 F.R.D. 209 (D. Del. 1957); *United States* v. *Janitz,* 161 F. 2d 19 (3d Cir. 1947). In a case such as this where the defendant is insane and in federal custody the Court has a special responsibility and authority over the proceedings, since such a defendant during commitment stands in the position of a ward of the Court. *United States* v. *Morris,* 154 F. Supp. 695 (S. D. Cal. 1957).

2. The motion presents an appeal to the discretion of the Court. For this reason, we ask leave to lodge the attached Statement of Robert Frost, who, along with many other poets and writers of distinction, has sought the release of Ezra Pound for the last several years. Although his statement does not speak to the legal issues raised, it is directly relevant to the serious considerations bearing upon this Court's exercise of its discretion.

Respectfully submitted,

THURMAN ARNOLD
WILLIAM D. ROGERS

STATEMENT OF ROBERT FROST SUBMITTED IN SUPPORT OF MOTION TO DISMISS INDICTMENT, APRIL 1958

I am here to register my admiration for a government that can rouse in conscience to a case like this. Relief seems in sight for many of us besides the Ezra Pound in question and his faithful wife. He has countless admirers the world over who will rejoice in the news that he has hopes of freedom. I append a page or so of what they have been saying lately about him and his predicament. I myself speak as much in the general interest as in his. And I feel authorized to speak very specially for my friends, Archibald MacLeish, Ernest Hemingway and T. S. Eliot. None of us can bear the disgrace of our letting Ezra Pound come to his end where he is. It would leave too woeful a story in American literature. He went very wrongheaded in his egotism, but he insists it was from patriotism—love of America. He has never admitted that he went over to the enemy any more than the writers at home who have despaired of the Republic. I hate such nonsense and can only listen to it as an evidence of mental disorder. But mental disorder is what we are considering. I rest the case on Dr. Overholser's pronouncement that Ezra Pound is not too dangerous to go free in his wife's care, and too insane ever to be tried—a very nice discrimination.

Mr. Thurman Arnold admirably put this problem of a sick man being held too long in prison to see if he won't get well enough to be tried for a prison offense. There is probably legal precedent to help toward a solution of the problem. But I should think it would have to be reached more by magnanimity than by logic and it is chiefly on magnanimity I am counting. I can see how the Department of Justice would hesitate in the matter from fear of looking more just to a great poet than it would be to a mere nobody. The bigger the Department the longer it might have to take thinking things through.

ROBERT FROST

STATEMENTS APPENDED TO ROBERT FROST'S STATEMENT OF APRIL, 1958

John Dos Passos:

"I certainly think he [Pound] should be released in the custody of his wife."

Van Wyck Brooks:

"I would gladly sign any petition for the release of Ezra Pound."

Marianne Moore:

"Yes indeed. I feel strongly that it is stagnant and unrealistic of us not to secure the release of Ezra Pound from St. Elizabeths."

Ernest Hemingway:

"Will gladly pay tribute to Ezra but what I would like to do is get him the hell out of St. Elizabeths . . ."

Carl Sandburg:

". . . they ought to let him out now; he's had enough."

W. H. Auden:

"There are very few living poets, even if they are not conscious of having been influenced by Pound, who could say, 'My work would be exactly the same if Mr. Pound had never lived.' "

T. S. Eliot:

"I believe that I have in the past made clear enough my personal debt to Ezra Pound during the years 1915-22. I have also expressed in several ways my opinion of his rank as a poet, as a critic, as impresario of other writers, and as pioneer of metric and poetic language. His 70th birthday is not a moment for qualifying one's praise, but merely for recognition of those services to literature, for which he will deserve the gratitude of posterity, and for appreciation of those achievements which even his severest critics must acknowledge."

Archibald MacLeish:

"Every year since I began teaching at Harvard and for long years before that I have been more impressed by the extraordinary vitality of Pound's work. Most work ages with time. His doesn't. It keeps the hard sharp glitter—the cutting edge."

Robert Fitzgerald:

"Ezra Pound's place in the story of poetry is not in question, and with every year, it becomes more discriminated and understood. . . . It goes without saying that all of us who practice the art of poetry are indebted to him."

Allen Tate:

"Pound is a great poet *in petto,* and an even greater instigator of literary enthusiasms and schools."

Dag Hammarskjöld:

"Modern art . . . makes us seers—seers like Ezra Pound when, in the first of his Pisan Cantos, he senses 'the enormous tragedy of the dream in the peasants' bent shoulders.' Seers—and explorers—these we must be if we are to prevail."

Richard H. Rovere:

"The main thing about Ezra Pound is that he is a poet of towering gifts and attainments. Poetry is not a horse race or any other sort of competition, and it is silly to argue over which poet runs the fastest, jumps the highest, or dives the deepest. Still, a respectable case could be made out to the effect that the century has produced no talent larger or more fecund than Pound's. Certainly the fit comparisons would be with no more than half a dozen other men who write in English. These, as the literary Establishment sees the matter today, would be T. S. Eliot, Yeats, Frost (some dissent here, probably), W. H. Auden and Dylan Thomas; later on, some of these names may be removed and replaced by some from the second rank, such as Wallace Stevens, Robert Graves, Walter de la Mare, Marianne Moore, William Carlos Williams, E. E. Cummings, and Robert Lowell.

"Pound's position is secure, not only because of the power of his own work but because of his service as a midwife to genius and as an influence on other poets. Not long ago, the government which detains Pound in St. Elizabeths circulated abroad, as part of its effort to persuade the world that we Americans really care about the finer things, a flossy periodical in which it was asserted that Ezra Pound 'has done more to serve the cause of English poetry than anyone else alive.' (The article, by Hayden Carruth, a gifted critic, also said, 'It is hard to think of a good reason why Pound should not have his freedom immediately.') The statement on his service is broad but difficult to gainsay. Of the poets of comparable stature, at least half have at one time or another been Pound's disciples; others were greatly aided by him. The best known and most influential poem of our time, Eliot's *The Waste Land,* took the shape in which the world knows it under his expert hand. Eliot submitted it to Pound at many stages, and in its penultimate stage it was, according to Eliot, 'a sprawling, chaotic poem . . . which left Pound's hands, reduced to about half its size, in the form in which it appears in print.' The dedication of *The Waste Land* reads, 'For Ezra Pound—*il miglior fabbro.*" Pound deeply influenced Yeats in the later phases of Yeats' career. But for Pound, the recognition of Robert Frost would have come more belatedly than it did. It was Pound who first got Frost published in the United States and Pound also who found a London publisher for James Joyce. Amy Lowell, E. E. Cummings, and William Carlos Williams sat, often in extreme discomfort, at his feet. W. H. Auden is of a later generation, but he has asserted that 'there are few living poets . . . who could say, "My work would be exactly the same if Mr. Pound had never lived." ' "

ORDER OF UNITED STATES DISTRICT COURT FOR THE DISTRICT OF COLUMBIA DISMISSING INDICTMENT

This cause came on for hearing on defendant's motion to dismiss the indictment and upon consideration of the affidavit of Dr. Winfred Overholser, the Superintendent of St. Elizabeths Hospital, and it appearing to the Court that the defendant is presently incompetent to stand trial and that there is no likelihood that this condition will in the foreseeable future improve, and it further appearing to the Court that there is available to the defense psychiatric testimony to the effect that there is a strong probability that the commission of the crimes charged was the result of insanity, and it appearing that the Government is not in a position to challenge this medical testimony, and it further appearing that the Government consents to the dismissal of this indictment, it is by the Court this 18th day of April, 1958,

ORDERED that the indictment be and the same is hereby dismissed.

BOLITHA J. LAWS
Chief Judge

NEW YORK TIMES, APRIL 19, 1958

WASHINGTON, April 18, 1958.—Treason charges against Ezra Pound were dismissed today, opening the way for the 72-year-old poet's return to Italy.

With the consent of the Government, Chief Judge Bolitha J. Laws of Federal District Court here threw out an indictment returned against Mr. Pound in 1945. The case was never tried because the poet was found insane.

Judge Laws acted on two psychiatric grounds—that Mr. Pound would in all likelihood never be mentally competent to stand trial and that the alleged radio broadcasts he had made from Italy during World War II might have been the result of insanity.

Medical advice to this effect had come from Dr. Winfred Overholser, superintendent of St. Elizabeths Hospital. That is the Federal mental institution where Mr. Pound has been confined since 1945. * * *

The court hearing today was a brief, formal affair, but with an undertone of drama.

Mr. Pound sat in the back of the courtroom, dressed in a shabby blue jacket, a tan sport shirt with the tails not tucked in and blue slacks. His pockets were full of folded envelopes and other scraps of paper.

Mrs. Pound and their son, Omar, a teacher at Roxbury Latin School in Boston, were with him, as were a group of persons evidently among his literary admirers. Mr. Pound would say nothing to reporters except a firm "yes" when asked if he wanted to return to Italy. He posed for pictures after putting on a long yellow scarf with Oriental characters on it.

Mr. Pound's attorney, Thurman Arnold, spoke for a few minutes, chiefly about Dr. Overholser's medical findings. He said he represented not only Mrs. Pound but also "the world community of poets and writers" in seeking dismissal of the indictment.

The Justice Department's representative, United States Attorney Oliver Gasch, said the Government thought the motion was "in the interest of justice and should be granted." He told Judge Laws, among other things, that it would be "virtually impossible" to produce evidence of Mr. Pound's sanity during the war years in Italy at so late a date. * * *

The person most responsible for today's denouement was not in court. He is Robert Frost, the poet, who had waged a persistent public and private campaign during the last two years for Mr. Pound's release. Among other things Mr. Frost had called on Attorney General William P. Rogers.

Soon afterward, Pound returned with his wife to Rapallo. He now lives in a flat at San Ambrogio, a tiny settlement in the hills overlooking Rapallo which is reached only by a mule track. The winter months find him in Venice. In between, he visits his daughter Mary and his grandchildren in their ancient castle in the Italian Alps near Merano.

Now eighty years of age, Pound is still physically vigorous. He was able to make a trip to London for the funeral of his dear friend, T. S. Eliot, and he accepted an invitation to be a guest of honor at the festival at Spoleto in 1965 where he received the acclaim of a brilliant assemblage of literary and artistic people. But the years have taken their toll. The old ebullience and fire have faded. Now there is the sweet, gentle, quiet old man, who is still writing what many consider the finest verse of our time.

APPENDIX

Appendix I

TEXT OF BROADCASTS

TRANSCRIPT OF SHORT WAVE BROADCAST, APRIL 23, 1942

The drift of Mr. Archibald MacLeish's remarks towards the end of March seems fairly clear. He has been given a gangster's brief and he has been entrusted with the defense of a gang of criminals and he is a-doing his damndest. I object and have objected to the crime, regardless of who may be related to the men who have committed it and I accept the conditions of the debate, namely that the Morgenthau-Lehman gang control 99% of all means of communication inside the United States and that they can drown out and buy out nearly all opposition, on top of which Roosevelt has, characteristically, resorted to blackmail. Any man who does not accept the gigantic frauds perpetrated by the Morgenthau-Roosevelt treasury is to be held up as a traitor to the United States.

The reply is that any man who submits to Roosevelt's treason to the public commits breach of citizen's duty. There is no connection between submittin' to the Roosevelt-Morgenthau frauds and patriotism. There is no connection between such submission and winning this war—or any other. There is no patriotism in submittin' to the prolonged and multiple frauds of the Roosevelt administration and to try to make the present support of these frauds figure as loyalty to the American Union, to the American Constitution, to the American heritage is just as much dirt or bunkum. Doubtless the tactics of evasion will be used to the uttermost, blackmail will be used to the uttermost—but if the American people submit to either or both of these wheezes the American people will be mugs.

There are several historic facts which the opulent of the Morgenthau-Lehman gang would do well to dig up. Our Mr. Mac-

Leish has not gone out—all out—for the printing of the defects of American history in handy and available volumes, so there are several historic facts which the opulent of the Morgenthau swindle would be well advised to extract and use.

Of course for you to go looking for my point—points of my bi-weekly talk in the maze of Jew-governed American radio transmissions—is like looking for one needle in a whole flock of hay stacks. And your press is not very open. However, if some lone watcher or listener on Back Bay or on top of the Blue Ridge does hear me, I suggest he make notes and ask Advocate Archibald whether it does win anything to have the people pay two dollars for every dollar spent by the government. I ask whether the spirit of '76 is helped by a-floodin' the lower ranks of the navy with bridge-sweepin's; whether war is won by mercantilist ethics and, in any case, whether men like Knox and Stimson and Morgenthau can be expected to fill the heart of youth with martial ardor and spirit of sacrifice.

I ask Archie to say openly why he handed out four billion dollars in excess profits on the gold . . . between 1932 and 1940, handing it to a dirty gang of kikes and hyper-kikes on the London gold exchange firms. Why is that expected to help Americanism? Or why should it be regarded as a model of devotion to the American spirits? Or why should any honest American vote for the continuance of that swindle or of keeping in office the men and kikes who were responsible for putting it over the people?

And that of course is not the whole story of Roosevelt, Lehman, Baruch, Morgenthau, dipping into the country's resources. The break with our tradition exemplified by Donovan's intrigues in Yugoslavia is no Cornelia's jewel. In fact, all Roosevelt's talk about patriotism is nothing but the gilding on the outside of base metal. Keeping Roosevelt in the White House is not essential to winning the war. The two things can be considered quite apart one from the other.

Had you had the sense to eliminate Roosevelt and his Jews or the Jews and their Roosevelt at the last election, you would not now be at war. That is one point. But to suppose that you will win the war by goin' on bein' mugs in any and every internal conflict, to suppose that you will strengthen the United States abroad by submittin' to continued internal bleedin' and swindlin' is just so much hokum or nonsense.

The first step towards a bright new world, so far as the rising American generation is concerned, is to git on to Roosevelt and all his works and the second is to eliminate him and all his damned gang from public life in America. The alternative is annihilation for the youth of America and the end of everything decent the U. S. ever stood for. If you allow yourself to be dazzled, if you are persuaded to identify the Morgenthau-Baruch-control of the U. S. by secret committees for the war birds with victory, then you are mugs. If you confuse these things and the promise of army contracts even with national defense, then you are plain downright suckers.

I shall be highly interested to see whether Archibald takes up any of the points of this discourse. If he don't, some bright lad ought to help him. Someone ought to dig up a point here or there.

TRANSCRIPT OF SHORT WAVE BROADCAST, MAY 15, 1943

Europe calling, Ezra Pound speaking.

About economic aggression. Mr. Sumner Welles' speech at Toledo was a serious matter. It is a great pity that even the majority of his listeners would have been unable to tell one at the end of it what he had said at the beginning. That is, it was a long and close exposition of argument, and at the mercy of even minor misunderstandings. It is a pity that auditors do not more often examine the printed text of such a speech. The efficiency of any communication can be further impaired when it falls to translators. In any case the minor shades fade out of language.

Who among the Toledo auditors now remembers whether Mr. Welles said that the subject, economic aggression, probably was, or ought to be in the minds of all of us. One Italian word* translates indifferently both the English phrase "next to" and the word

* Dopo.

"after." I mean, that is, when the translation is verbally correct at one point but does not take into account the whole paragraph.

Had I been making a daily or immediate comment, I might have drawn rash conclusions or no conclusions whatever. The man reporting on the events of the day hasn't time to chew over the text and place it on a general scheme. Probably few among you thought of correlating the Welles' speech with a talk, made a week before by Mr. Ager, speaking from London on the B. B. C. and allegedly connected with the American Embassy. Had Mr. Welles been ready to make such a speech three years ago, this distressing war might have been quite well avoided. Mr. Welles appeared to be renouncing dollar diplomacy. A few months sooner, a good deal of bloodshed might have been spared us. Mr. Welles also spoke of misapprehension, of incomplete knowledge, of heedlessness, inconsideration.

I'm perfectly ready to take Mr. Welles' speech at its face value. If the United States has been ill informed, or tardily informed of the conditions of Europe, there is no reason for you to remain voluntarily in that condition. But, it is now extremely hard for the people inside any country to get accurate impressions of the state of mind of people inside any other. It has been for years, extremely hard to get news into America. I have long held that more disinterested observers, American observers, should be let loose in Europe. I mean people whose news and views is not limited by what they can sell to the advertiser of a particular paper or group of papers. Undeniably, misunderstandings have arisen and still arise, and will continue to arise until it is profitable for people to talk without hate, and without attempting to read into other men's statements what the speaker or writer never intended to put there. I mean, that is the question of will, a question of good will. Of being ready to hear what the other man says to you. It is not to be supposed that even now, Mr. Welles would listen to me over a cable, or answer what I intend to say to him during the next five minutes.

I have been trying to get news of Europe across the Atlantic for a number of years, it is today my impression that Mr. Welles was speaking of a Germany which no longer exists. I know that for years the American people were incited against an Italy which was not the Italy that I live in. Before all wars, before any war, there arises a tide of misrepresentation. That sort of thing did not begin in this century or the last one. In every country there are groups of people who aim at construction. They toil more or less consecutively to ameliorate living conditions. They are often considered impractical. Sometimes they get into office. There are also in all countries, destructive or heedless groups.

Sometimes heedless, sometimes also malevolent. Now to the outer world, the American history of the past 30 years appears to be an uninterrupted record of economic aggression on the part of the United States. The United States is the hometown of the Rockefellers, Guggenheims, Morgan. The world has had on its news stalls the works of Vishka (?), I suppose he's a Polish author. Anyhow he wrote the "War for Oil," "War for Cotton," and so on. And we have heard of wars for commodities and wars for gold. We have heard much less of a sacred war that the United States lost in 1863.

While the boys in blue and the boys in grey were obligingly dying and taking the spotlight, the Civil War was, at that time, a world record for carnage and both sides well vanquished. The control of the national credit, control of the national currency, the national purchasing power, passes right away from the people and right out of the control of the national and responsible government. That is why many of Mr. Welles' foreign auditors will think there is a nigger in Mr. Welles' woodshed. Suddenly a coalition of the three most aggressive powers, economically aggressive powers, on earth, put forth not an official statement, but a statement by the most authoritative member of the State Department to the effect that economic aggression is, after all, a factor in causing wars, and that to obtain a durable peace we must lay off it.

England, Mr. Welles tell us, is aggressive, economically. The United States, has in the past been aggressive, Russia has made up for lost time and been extremely aggressive. Quite economically. It does sound to the European almost as if Legs Diamond, or Billy the Kid or Jesse James had suddenly decided to change his habits. I mean, economic aggression has been for so long considered the very breath of life for the American system, the bone of its bone, its inner and intimate fiber. And then again, when a nation's inner life is so palpably made up of the economic aggression of one class or group against the whole rest of the population, it is very difficult for any foreigner, or indeed for anyone not carried away by political heat of the moment, to see why that particular nation should be entrusted with the latch key of any other.

I will return to this subject.

Ezra Pound, speaking.

Appendix II

TEXT OF THE INDICTMENT

In the District Court of the United States
for the District of Columbia

October Term A.D. 1945

The Grand Jurors for the United States of America duly impaneled and sworn in the District Court of the United States for the District of Columbia and inquiring for that District upon their oath present:

1. That Ezra Pound, the defendant herein, was born at Hailey, Idaho, October 30, 1885, and that he has been at all times herein mentioned and now is a citizen of the United States of America and a person owing allegiance to the United States of America.

2. That the defendant, Ezra Pound, at Rome, Italy and other places within the kingdom of Italy and outside the jurisdiction of any particular state or district, but within the jurisdiction of the United States and of this Court, the District of Columbia being the district in which he was found and into which he was first brought, continuously, and at all times beginning on the 11th day of December 1941, and continuing thereafter to and including the 3rd day of May 1945, under the circumstances and conditions and in the manner and by the means hereinafter set forth, then and there being a citizen of the United States, and a person owing allegiance to the United States, in violation of said duty of allegiance, knowingly, intentionally, wilfully, unlawfully, feloniously, traitorously and treasonably did adhere to the enemies of the United States, to-wit; the Kingdom of Italy and the military allies of the said Kingdom of

Italy, with which the United States at all times since December 11, 1941, and during the times set forth in this indictment, have been at war, giving to the said enemies of the United Sates aid and comfort within the United States and elsewhere, that is to say:

3. That the aforesaid adherence of the said defendant, Ezra Pound, to the Kingdom of Italy and its military allies and the giving of aid and comfort by the said defendant, Ezra Pound, to the aforesaid enemies of the United States during the time aforesaid consisted:

(a) Of accepting employment from the Kingdom of Italy in the capacity of a radio propagandist and in the performance of the duties thereof which involved the composition of texts, speeches, talks and announcements and the recording thereof for subsequent broadcast over short-wave radio on wave lengths audible in the United States and elsewhere on ordinary commercial radio receiving sets having short-wave reception facilities; and

(b) Of counselling and aiding the Kingdom of Italy and its military allies and proposing and advocating to the officials of the Government of the Kingdom of Italy ideas and thoughts, as well as methods by which such ideas and thoughts could be disseminated, which the said defendant, Ezra Pound, believed suitable and useful to the Kingdom of Italy for propaganda purposes in the prosecution of said war;

That the aforesaid activities of the said defendant, Ezra Pound, were intended to persuade citizens and residents of the United States to decline to support the United States in the conduct of the said war, to weaken or destroy confidence in the Government of the United States and in the integrity and loyalty of the Allies of the United States, and to further bind together and increase the morale of the subjects of the Kingdom of Italy in support of the prosecution of the said war by the Kingdom of Italy and its military allies.

4. And the Grand Jurors aforesaid upon their oath aforesaid do further present that the said defendant, Ezra Pound, in the prosecution, performance and execution of said treason and of said unlawful, traitorous and treasonable adhering and giving aid and comfort to the enemies of the United States, at the several times hereinafter set forth in the specifications hereof (being times when

the United States were at war with the Kingdom of Italy and its military allies), unlawfully, feloniously, wilfully, knowingly, traitorously and treasonably and with intent to adhere to and give aid and comfort to the said enemies, did do, perform, and commit certain overt and manifest acts, that is to say:

> (Here the indictment alleges overt acts consisting of broadcasts by Pound over a radio station of the Italian government at Rome, Italy on September 11, 1942; December 10, 1942; February 4, 1943; March 19, 1943; May 12, 1943; May 14, 1943; May 15, 1943; and recording of broadcasts on various dates.)

16. On or about July 11, 1942, the said defendant, Ezra Pound, for the purpose of giving aid and comfort to the Kingdom of Italy and its then allies in the war against the United States, accepted and received payment and remuneration in the sum of 700 lire from the Kingdom of Italy for compiling and recording messages, speeches and talks for subsequent broadcast to the United States and elsewhere from a radio station in Rome, Italy.

17. Between December 11, 1941 and May 3, 1945, the said defendant, Ezra Pound, for the purpose of giving aid and comfort to the Kingdom of Italy and its then allies in the war against the United States, on a day and date to these Grand Jurors unknown, accepted and received payment and remuneration from the Kingdom of Italy in an amount to these Grand Jurors unknown, for compiling and recording messages, speeches and talks for subsequent broadcast to the United States and elsewhere from a radio station in Rome, Italy.

18. On or about June 24, 1942, the said defendant, Ezra Pound, for the purpose of giving aid and comfort to the Kingdom of Italy and its then allies in the war against the United States, accepted and received payment and remuneration in the sum of 350 lire, from the Kingdom of Italy for compilation of notes and comments for broadcast to the United States and elsewhere from a radio station located in the Kingdom of Italy.

19. Between December 11, 1941 and May 3, 1945, the said defendant, Ezra Pound, for the purpose of giving aid and comfort to the Kingdom of Italy and its then allies in the war against the

United States, on a day and date to these Grand Jurors unknown, accepted and received payment and remuneration from the Kingdom of Italy in an amount to these Grand Jurors unknown, for compilation of notes and comments for broadcast to the United States and elsewhere from a radio station located in the Kingdom of Italy.

The defendant, Ezra Pound, committed each and every one of the overt acts herein described for the purpose of, and with the intent to adhere to and give aid and comfort to the Kingdom of Italy, and its military allies, enemies of the United States, and the said defendant, Ezra Pound, committed each and every one of the said overt acts contrary to his duty of allegiance to the United States and to the form of the statute and constitution in such case made and provided and against the peace and dignity of the United States. (Section 1, United States Criminal Code.)

A True Bill

Appendix III

BRIEF CONCERNING BAIL

MEMORANDUM OF LAW ON APPLICATION FOR BAIL, SUBMITTED NOVEMBER 27, 1945 TO THE UNITED STATES DISTRICT COURT FOR THE DISTRICT OF COLUMBIA

This memorandum is submitted in support of the defendant's application for admission to bail pending trial on the indictment and is confined to a discussion of the law bearing upon the application, the facts being set forth in a separate affidavit of defendant's counsel, Julien Cornell.

The Indictment

The defendant was indicted at a criminal term held July 1943, of the District Court of the United States for the District of Columbia, upon presentation of the Grand Jury of the District charging him with having committed the crime of treason in violation of Section 1 of the United States Criminal Code, by the transmission of certain broadcasts over a radio station at Rome, Italy, in which it is alleged that he, being a United States citizen, and owing allegiance to the United States, adhered and gave aid and counsel to an enemy state, namely, the Kingdom of Italy. The defendant having not yet been furnished with a copy of the indictment, and the full text not being available to counsel, the indictment is not here set forth.

The defendant's counsel is informed and believes that a superseding indictment has been, or will soon be requested by the Department of Justice alleging the same crime and on substantially the same grounds.

Constitutional Provisions

The crime of treason is the only crime which, because of its importance in Colonial times, was defined in the Constitution of the United States.

> "Treason against the United States, shall consist only in levying War against them, or in adhering to their Enemies, giving them Aid and Comfort. No Person shall be convicted of Treason unless on the Testimony of two Witnesses to the same overt Act, or on Confession in open Court." (U. S. Constitution, Art. 3, Sec. 3.)

Statutory Provisions

The definition of the crime of treason is also contained in the Criminal Code in language derived from the constitutional provision.

> "(*Criminal Code, section 1.*) *Treason.* Whoever, owing allegiance to the United States, levies war against them or adheres to their enemies, giving them aid and comfort within the United States or elsewhere, is guilty of treason." (R.S. Sec. 5331; Mar. 4, 1909, c. 321, Sec. 1, 35 Stat. 1088.) (18 U. S. Code, Sec. 1)

The punishment for treason is specified in Sec. 2 of the Criminal Code.

> "Whoever is convicted of treason shall suffer death; or, at the discretion of the court, shall be imprisoned not less than five years and fined not less than $10,000. to be levied on and collected out of any or all of his property, real and personal, of which he was the owner at the time of committing such treason, any sale or conveyance to the contrary notwithstanding and every person so convicted of treason shall, moreover, be incapable of holding any office under the United States." (R.S. Sec. 5332; Mar. 4, 1909, c. 321, Sec. 2, 35 Stat. 1088.) (18 U.S.C. Sec. 2)

Admission to bail is expressly permitted by statute in all capital offenses. (The crime of treason is a capital offense—Criminal Code Sec. 2 supra.)

> "Bail may be admitted upon all arrests in criminal cases where the punishment may be death; but in such cases it shall be taken only by the Supreme Court or a circuit court, or by a justice of the Supreme Court, a circuit judge, or a judge of a district court, who shall exercise their discretion therein, having regard to the nature and circumstance of the offense, and of the evidence, and to the usages of law." (R.S. Sec. 1016; 18 U.S.C. Sec. 597.)

Argument

A defendant accused of treason may be admitted to bail while awaiting trial within the discretion of the court.

As expressly provided in the statute set forth in full above "bail may be admitted upon all arrests in criminal cases where the punishment may be death" and bail may be taken by a district court or by a judge thereof "who shall exercise their discretion therein, having regard to the nature and circumstances of the offense and of the evidence, and to the usages of law." (18 U.S.C. Sec. 597, as made applicable to district courts by Act of March 3, 1911, 36 Stat. 1167.)

As provided by Sec. 2 of the Criminal Code, 18 U.S.C. Sec. 2, punishment for treason may be death or a fine and imprisonment at the discretion of the court. These statutes taken together expressly provide, therefore, that a defendant arrested on a charge of treason may be admitted to bail while awaiting trial, and that such bail may be taken by a district court or judge thereof, in his discretion, having regard to (1) the nature and circumstances of the offense, (2) the evidence against the defendant, and (3) usages of law. Discretion with regard to the granting of bail exists only in capital cases, as in all other cases the allowance of bail is mandatory. (18 U.S.C. 597.)

The crime of treason is so rare in our recent history that there is little precedent in the way of usage by which the court may be guided. Defendant's counsel has not had an opportunity to examine all the cases involving treason in recent years, to determine whether bail has been sought or permitted in any of them. The only treason case which has reached the United States Supreme Court in modern times is *Cramer* v. *U. S.,* 325 U. S. 1. Although the opinions do not shed any light on the matter of bail, they may prove helpful as containing the only authoritative discussion of the crime, as well as a learned review of its history in English and American law.

It was established very early in the history of the United States that the crime of treason is bailable under the statutes. In the case of *U. S.* v. *Hamilton,* 3 Dallas 17 (1795), the United States Supreme Court issued a writ of habeas corpus on the petition of a prisoner who had been arrested on the warrant of a district judge, charged with the crime of high treason, in that he aided insurrectionists by attending their meetings. The prisoner had been committed to jail without any hearing and he not only requested that he be properly arraigned, but also that he be admitted to bail. Despite the fact that the man was accused not merely of propaganda, but of actual aid to a rebellious group within the United States, the Supreme Court directed that he be admitted to bail until the trial and fixed the bail in the sum of $4,000 with two sureties for $2,000 each. In another capital case, this one involving the crime of piracy, Hon. Bushrod Washington, Associate Justice of the Supreme Court, sitting in the Circuit Court for the District of Pennsylvania, admitted the defendant to bail. *U. S.* v. *Jones,* Fed. Cas. No. 15496 (1813).

In the latter case, Justice Washington in admitting the defendant to bail in the sum of $10,000 stated that he granted bail because the defendant was ill and continued imprisonment would be harmful to him, although there was no immediate or certain danger that he would die if not released.

> "As to Jones, it is proved by the physician who has attended him since February, in jail, that his health is bad, his complaint pulmonary, and that, in his opinion, confinement during the summer might so far increase his disorder as to render it ultimately dangerous. The humanity of our laws, not less than the feelings of the court, favor the liberation

> of a prisoner upon bail, under such circumstances. It is not necessary, in our view of the subject, that the danger which may arise from his confinement should be either immediate or certain. If, in the opinion of a skilful physician, the nature of his disorder is such that confinement must be injurious, and may be fatal, we think he ought to be bailed."

If Justice Washington had no compunctions about applying rules of humanity to a man accused of piracy, and suffering only from a physical ailment, this court has ample precedent for admitting to bail Ezra Pound, who has been charged with a crime hardly more heinous than piracy, and not only appears to be insane at the present time, as a result of previous imprisonment, but may very likely be rendered permanently insane, and may lose his life, if imprisonment continues.

Respectfully submitted,

JULIEN CORNELL
Attorney for Defendant

Appendix IV

TRANSCRIPT OF TRIAL

TRANSCRIPT OF HEARING IN THE UNITED STATES DISTRICT COURT FOR THE DISTRICT OF COLUMBIA, FEBRUARY 13, 1946

The Clerk of the Court: The case of Ezra Pound.

The Court: Swear the jury.

The Clerk of the Court: The jurors will stand and raise your right hands.

(Thereupon, the jurors were sworn on *voir dire.*)

The Court: Members of the jury, the case which the jury will be impanelled to hear is one involving Ezra Pound, who is the defendant in a criminal case pending in this Court.

Mr. Pound is seated here. Will you stand, Mr. Pound, and face the jury?

Thank you.

Certain representations have been made to the Court that Mr. Pound is not in mental condition such as that he is able to participate with counsel in the trial of a criminal case, and is not in position to understand the full nature of the charges against him.

Based upon that showing which has been made to me by psychiatrists, I am going to impanel a jury to pass upon that question. In the event the jury finds that his mental state is as has been represented to me, then Mr. Pound will not be brought to trial because, under the law, it would not be proper to prosecute him if his mental condition is as has been stated to me.

Now appearing for Mr. Pound is Mr. Julien Cornell of New York. Will you stand, please?

Representing the United States Government in this case is Mr. Matlack and Mr. Donald Anderson from the Department of Justice, who are now facing you.

Do any of you know Mr. Pound?

Juror Wingfield: I do.

The Court: What is your name?

Juror Wingfield: John Wingfield.

The Court: How long have you known him?

Juror Wingfield: Ever since he has been there in the hospital.

The Court: Do you know some of the facts with reference to this matter?

Juror Wingfield: Yes.

The Court: I will excuse you from this case.

Do any of the others know Mr. Pound?

Have any of you heard any of his broadcasts?

Do any of you know Mr. Cornell?

Do any of you know counsel for the United States, Mr. Matlack or Mr. Anderson?

Does any one of you know any reason why you cannot render a fair and impartial verdict in a matter of this type?

Has any member of your family, or any close friend, or have any of you been involved in any proceeding to attack their sanity?

Have you any further questions?

Mr. Matlack: We are satisfied.

Mr. Cornell: I would like Your Honor to ask the jury in view of the fact that this defendant broadcast statements during war-time in which he was highly critical of our Government, and also some statements which might be construed as anti-Semitic, whether they could render an impartial verdict?

The Court: Would any of you be prejudiced by reason of the fact that Mr. Pound made broadcasts that are said to have been against our Government, or against the Jewish race?

The question here is solely one of sanity of this particular individual, and under our law a man should not be brought to trial if he is in the condition they say he is, and it would be your duty to render a fair and impartial verdict in that case.

Is there any doubt in your mind about that?

The Court: Are you satisfied with the jury, Mr. Matlack?

Mr. Matlack: Yes, sir.

The Court: Mr. Cornell?

Mr. Cornell: I am satisfied.

The Court: Swear the jury.

(Thereupon, the above-named jury was sworn by the Clerk of the Court.)

Mr. Cornell: Call Dr. Muncie.

Thereupon Dr. WENDELL MUNCIE, a witness called on behalf of the Defendant, being first duly sworn, was examined and testified as follows:

The Clerk of the Court: Be seated, please, and state your full name.

The Witness: Dr. Wendell Muncie.

Direct Examination by Mr. Cornell:

Q. Dr. Muncie, will you state your profession? A. I am a psychiatrist.

Q. Will you tell me what institutions you are connected with in your practice? A. Johns Hopkins Hospital, Baltimore; Marine Hospital, Baltimore; Eaton Institute, Baltimore; and Mt. Alto. I am Associate Professor of Psychiatry at the Johns Hopkins Hospital, and consulting psychiatrist in other hospitals.

Q. How long have you been engaged in the practice of medicine and psychiatry? A. In the practice of medicine since 1927, and in psychiatry since 1929.

Q. What hospital are you a graduate from? A. Johns Hopkins.

Q. Have you written any books or papers on psychiatry? A. A number of papers and a text book.

Q. Is that book still used in the practice of psychiatry? A. Well, it still sells.

Q. In the practice of your profession have you had occasion to engage in the examination of the sanity of people? A. That is all I do, and treat them.

Q. On an average, how many persons whose sanity is in question do you see during a year? A. I spend about 2200 hours either examining patients or treating patients in the course of a year, and in that time I suppose of those 2200 hours 500 of them represent new patients, maybe more.

Q. In the course of those investigations do you have occasion to investigate all types of mental disorders? A. Yes, sir.

Q. Will you tell me, Dr. Muncie, when did you first examine the defendant here, Mr. Pound? A. December 13, 1945.

Q. At that time he was already under indictment for this crime, as you have been informed, is that right? A. Yes, sir.

Q. And where was he then confined? A. He was in the Gallinger Hospital.

Q. Did you perform this examination in collaboration with any other physician? A. Part of it was with the other three psychiatrists, but most of it I made myself.

Q. By the other three psychiatrists, do you mean those three doctors out there who are witnesses in this case? A. Yes.

Q. Were you attempting to define his illness? A. Yes.

Q. Will you state what symptoms you found in Mr. Pound? A. Yes sir. May I have reference to some notes?

Q. Certainly. Perhaps you had better turn to the jury so they can hear you clearly. A. There are a number of things which attracted my attention in examining Mr. Pound, and these are essentially the items that appeared to me:

He has a number of rather fixed ideas which are either clearly delusional or verging on the delusional. One I might speak of, for instance, he believes he has been designated to save the Constitution of the United States for the people of the United States.

I will come back to this item in a minute.

Secondly, he has a feeling that he has the key to the peace of the world through the writings of Confucius, which he translated into Italian and into English, and that if this book had been given proper circulation the Axis would not have been formed, we would be at peace now, and a great deal of trouble could have been avoided in the past, and this becomes his blueprint for world order in the future.

Third, he believes that with himself as a leader, a group of intellectuals could have gotten together in different countries, like Japan, for instance, where he is well thought of, to work for world order. He has a hatred of bureaucrats which goes back a long way, and one may conclude that his saving of the Constitution draws a clear distinction between the rights of the people and those who govern people.

He feels he was double-crossed in being brought back to this country, thinking that he was being brought back to aid the country because of his special connections in Italy, and that his double-cross was at the hands of the British Commandos.

So much for the rather fixed ideas he holds.

In addition to that, he shows a remarkable grandiosity. He feels that he has no peer in the intellectual field, although conceding that one or two persons he has assisted might, on occasion, do as good work as he did.

This grandiosity I speak of, in connection with the translation of Confucius, he thinks might have prevented the formation of the Axis, and if he could only get to Japan and work through the poets over there he could work for world order.

This all sounds as if it was clear-cut. Quite the contrary, it is not clear-cut, and the case from any psychiatric picture has a remarkable vagueness and when one attempts to follow his exposition of these vague ideas I, at least, have been left out on a limb every time. I would say he is unable to make a solution of his own fixed ideas, and he cannot explain or balance the significance of the difficulty in his thinking operations.

In addition to the vagueness, there is a considerable distractibility, as we call it, that is to say, he moves from topic to topic; for instance, if he is asked a specific question as to a specific situation he begins to make an answer and then all of a sudden is making a statement about a number of topics which may be clear in his mind but cannot be clear in the examiner's mind. There is a great push, and then a condition which we refer to as stupor when nothing comes. He just holds his head and nothing comes, and at those times he has complained of a feeling of emptiness in the forehead, or a feeling of pressure in the forehead also, and I did see an interesting phenomenon on one occasion:

The first time I saw him, December 13th, I referred in a social way to the fact that my brother had been a student at Wabash College, where he spent some six months in connection with his post-graduate career. He obviously did not remember my brother and the matter was passed off lightly. When I saw him on January 7th I was reintroduced to him by the other doctors, and his immediate comment was, "Yes, you have a brother," and "he was my best student, he had just come back from Europe, and he came from a family of the highest culture in Indiana."

Now, irrespective of the merits of this latter issue, this is pure confabulation; I would say it is a confusion of facts in the face of real lack of memory about my brother. It is the only item I had that I could corroborate, although there may be other examples of confabulation. He complains of exhaustion as the cause of his breakdown in—

Q. Before you go on, Doctor, will you explain the cause of confabulation? A. Confabulation may have a number of causes, with no ulterior motive, but ordinarily when we use the term, and I would think very strongly in that connection, it is occasioned by a definite loss of memory, and it usually appears in people with some kind of deteriorating process of the brain. I did not stress this point too much because it was just one item, and not necessary to my understanding of the case.

He believes the exhaustion is the cause of the breakdown in his thinking processes. His memory definitely is not keen. It takes time for the answer to come.

Now, in addition to these things which represent to my mind the formal aspects of the disorder in the thinking process, vagueness, distractibility and confabulation, and the poor, not keen, memory, and things coming back very slowly, he definitely shows a very poor grasp of his present situation.

He felt, he tells me, that he was being brought back to this country to help the Government in understanding the Italian situation, and to work towards the rehabilitation of the world. He apparently did not realize that he was being brought back here for treason, and when he found that out his argument was that he must have been double-crossed and that it was, as I said, at the hands of the British Intelligence Service or Commandos.

That is how the patient appears to me, and it may not be necessary to go into further diagnosis.

Q. Doctor, I would like for you to go into a little more detail about his predicament, and how well he understands it. A. He has two minds about that. At times he believes he could persuade any jury who could understand him of the fact that he had not committed treason. At other times, he states categorically that he is not of sound mind and could not participate effectively in his own defense. The latter I would concur with.

Q. Did you at any time ascertain whether he understood the nature of the offense? A. Whether he understands the meaning of treason, or not, I do not know. He categorically denies that he committed anything like treason, in his mind, against the people of the United States.

Q. Were you able to discuss it with him sufficiently to find out whether or not he had any grasp of the nature of his alleged crime? A. Such discussions, and there have been several, always end up in bringing in all the matters I talked about, the economic situation, Confucius, Japan, and so forth, but by no stretch of the imagination can you make him realize the seriousness of his predicament, and that is the astonishing thing, if you touch on his case and hospitalization, Confucius and these other things seemed to get roped in, and you end up with a confusion of thought.

Q. In other words, he is not able to pursue a point logically, but he does confuse it with other ideas, is that right? A. Yes.

Q. Were you able to discover whether any other mental difficulties had occurred in his previous life? A. Well, all we know is from the record that he went through an unusual mental experience in a concentration camp in Italy, which, by all the records, must have been a profound emotional experience amounting, I suppose, to a panic state, but to suggest how it might be described technically, I don't know. But it was a rather severe emotional crisis he went through, at which time he was seen, I think, by some psychiatrists.

Q. Before that did you examine sufficient of his writings, and so on, to be able to determine whether or not this condition may have arisen in his earlier life? A. I have read a great deal of his writings in connection with preparing this case, and it is my idea that there has been for a number of years a deterioration of the mental processes.

Q. Will you tell the jury what is your opinion as to Mr. Pound's ability to understand the meaning of a trial under this indictment for treason, and particularly his ability to consult with counsel and formulate a defense to the indictment? A. I think he is not capable of doing any of those things.

Q. Would you think that your opinion would become more clear by giving it in medical diagnostic terminology, Dr. Muncie, or doesn't that add anything to the picture? A. I don't think it does. Those are of a statistical nature. I would say in ordinary language he has been a peculiar individual for many, many years, and that on top of that in recent years, I don't know how long back, he has been engrossed with these things I have talked about as neurotic developments. For statistical purposes we could call this a paranoid condition.

Q. By "paranoid" do I understand that involves delusions and self-aggrandizement? A. Yes.

Q. Do you know whether Mr. Pound in his present condition would be able to stand up under the rigors of a cross-examination? A. That is predicting things into the future, and one cannot predict, but I think it would be rather dangerous to his welfare.

Mr. Matlack: If the Court please, I have no objection to the questions, but I do not think this should take into consideration what he might do in the future.

The Court: Well, if it was of today it would be all right.

If he were to go on trial at the present time, Doctor, do you think his nervous system would be able to sustain him throughout the trial?

The Witness: I think it would be very doubtful, very hazardous.

Mr. Cornell: No more questions.

Cross-Examination by Mr. Matlack:

Q. How many times, Doctor, did you see Mr. Pound? A. Twice. December 13th and February 7th.

Q. How long a period did you talk to him? A. The first time between three and four hours, the second time two hours.

Q. During the time you saw Mr. Pound December 13th, which you say was a period of three hours— A. Practically, yes.

Q. How much of that time did you talk to him alone? A. Most of the time, all but about 15 minutes.

Q. And the rest of the time by yourself after introduction by the other doctors? A. Yes.

Q. Did you go into his history when you went to interview him? A. I had a statement from Mr. Cornell of Mr. Pound's situation up to the date of his being taken prisoner in Italy and being brought back here.

Q. Did you have any history back of that? A. I had excerpts from newspapers, and from people who are in better position to judge his literary ability.

Q. By newspaper articles you refer to those contained in the petition filed here? A. Yes.

Q. Did you have any other history given to you by Mr. Pound as to his condition? A. No, sir.

Q. Did you have any information furnished to you by Mr. Pound as to where he was born, for instance? A. Oh, I had secondary information to which I had access, hospital records at Gallinger, which was rather complete.

Q. Did you consider his past life from the time he left the United States? A. At considerable length.

Q. Was he able to discuss that intelligently with you? A. Well, he gave me some of the facts.

Q. And did he give them to you correctly as the hospital record showed? A. I think so.

Q. Did he have any loss of memory as to his past history? A. He said that there was a period of three to four years preceding the Italian capture, not capture, but since he gave himself up to the American Army, that he is not sure about the allocation of events in time. I have no way of corroborating that. That may or may not be true.

Q. Is he able to correlate events in the last four or five years in all ordinary particulars? A. It would depend on the events, I think.

Q. Do you know what events he was referring to? A. No, it was nothing that I could check up on so I did not pursue it any further.

Q. What bearing did Pound's history, as given to you by him have upon your diagnosis? A. It has this bearing, that I think it gives indisputable proof of a peculiar personality for many years. That is the basis for my diagnosis of the paranoid make-up.

Q. Let me ask you this: Do you think a peculiar personality denotes insanity? A. No, not in the strict sense of the term.

Q. Do you think that the peculiar personality that you say he has—I presume that is from your impression from talking to him—prevents him from properly understanding the charge that he has been charged with and prevents him from discussing the matter with his counsel? A. That doesn't, but that is not all of the diagnosis. That is the background diagnosis. The present situation is something else, as I have indicated.

Q. Now, what was the nature of the examination you gave Mr. Pound during the time you saw him? A. A psychiatric examination. It is a recital and examination of material that you can check on today, I would say, by direct examination, having to do with his mental content, or his thought, his type of thinking process and his intellectual capacity.

Q. I think it might be of help to the jury, I know it would to me, if you would tell us a little more in detail what a psychiatric examination consists of. A. There are two aspects; you give the patient a chance to state spontaneously anything he wants to state which he thinks relevant to his complaint, spontaneously going to great lengths and bringing in a great deal of material which may or may not be relevant to the present situation. After you have satisfied yourself about his understanding of the situation, and the material he would like to produce about it, then you begin to ask specific questions to satisfy yourself on those things, whether his mentality is out of order, and his intellectual resources are out of order, or whether his thinking processes are out of order.

These questions have to do with material that you can check on, current events, retention of thought, and so forth.

Q. How did you find his memory? A. His memory, as far as I could find was all right, except for a substantial period in the concentration camp where there appears to have been a blackout of memory.

Q. That would not be unusual, in your opinion, Doctor, under such stress or strain? A. It is unusual when related to the emotional panic which he experienced there at that concentration camp, and to which concentration he was not used to.

Q. Don't you think it is rather normal for a person subsequently arrested for a charge of treason to be under great emotional stress? A. I wouldn't know, Mr. Matlack. One might suppose that would be an incentive to keep your thoughts about you. The answer is, I don't know.

Q. Have you had occasion to examine many cases of people who are under criminal charges? A. Not many. I have had occasion to but I haven't done it.

Q. So you don't know whether being under a criminal charge causes emotional stress? A. I know they write books on that topic.

Q. Did you give any consideration to the writings and publications of Mr. Pound in coming to your conclusions? A. Not as to his broadcast subjects. A man has to try to understand the background of his personality. I think one would have to.

Q. Has the nature of the charge, namely, that of treason, had anything to do with it, in your opinion? A. No, sir.

Q. In other words, what I have in mind is that if the charge had been something less than treason, say embezzlement, something of that sort, which did not relate to his writings and broadcasts, would your opinion be that his mental condition would be different than you found it to be? A. No, that has nothing to do with it.

Q. You do not think that the charge itself relating to writing, or his broadcasts which is, of course, in his line of endeavor, namely, writing, would have any bearing? A. As far as I am able to judge in the case, I would say no.

Q. Now, you say he had fixed ideas, if I understood you correctly, and the first one was that he thought he had an assigned task to save the Constitution. Do you think that in itself indicates any inability to consult with counsel and to understand the charge he is charged with? A. No.

Q. There are a lot of people, aren't there, with certain fixed ideas that we, as laymen, may think are peculiar, which do not in themselves indicate insanity? A. Yes.

Q. And your second statement, correct me if I am wrong, is that he believes he has the key to the peace of the world through the translations of Confucius, and that if the world had listened to him in that respect there would not have been any formation of the Axis? A. Yes.

Q. Would that in itself make you say that he was insane? A. No.

Q. And then I think you said the third thing was that he felt, with himself as leader, if a group of intellectuals could have gotten together with certain poets, or other people, in Japan and possibly elsewhere, that they could have arrived at a solution of some kind of peace, but that they did not do it? A. Yes.

Q. Does that indicate insanity? A. It indicates to my mind that he is getting farther and farther away from the reality of the situation. Whether that in itself constitutes insanity I would say no, one is entitled to some queer ideas without being called insane.

Q. And then I think you said he had a hatred of bureaucrats. I think a lot of people have that, don't they? A. Yes.

Q. And that, in itself, would not necessarily indicate that he was insane? A. That's right.

Q. And the fifth fixed idea, as I take it, is that he feels he was double-crossed in being brought back to this country, that he thought he was being brought back to consult about Italy but found he was charged with treason? A. Yes.

Q. Did you talk to him about this charge of treason at all? A. Yes.

Q. Did he tell you that he had been indicted in 1943 as a result of his broadcasts? A. No, that came to him as a surprise later on.

Q. But he did know it before he was brought back to this country? A. I think he did.

Q. And did he know that he was placed in a concentration camp because of those charges? A. No, he said he turned himself in to the American forces voluntarily because of his knowledge concerning Italy.

Q. And that was his explanation, I mean he did not vary from that at all? A. No, that was his explanation.

Q. When did he say he learned that he was charged with treason? A. I really don't know that.

Q. At the time you examined him in December, did you think that there was any question in his mind that he was charged with treason? A. Oh, no, he knew it then.

Q. Do you think he understood what treason was? A. Well, I think he does.

Q. Do you think he understands the nature of the charge, and that possibly he would be tried for the crime of treason? A. Yes.

Q. Now, what do you mean, Doctor, when you say he shows grandiosity? What does that mean? A. It means an exaggerated opinion of one's self.

Q. Is that a sign of insanity? A. If it gets out of bounds it is.

Q. When does it get out of bounds, in your opinion? A. It gets out of bounds in certain paranoid states, and in certain minor conditions which I do not think enter into the picture.

By the Court:

Q. That is very common to paranoia, isn't it? A. Yes.

By Mr. Matlack:

Q. What is paranoia? A. Paranoia is a mental state in which there is a fixed state of delusion with logical inferences resting on an untenable hypothesis. If one grants as reasonable the hypothesis, then all the rest of the system of ideas must be true. Pure paranoia is rare. There is logical thinking, and you cannot therefore refute his ideas if you admit his original premise.

The finding here is that all ideas are fixed in the sense that he comes back to them all the time, but none of them is clear. It is all vague. That is the essential difference.

Q. You mean vague to the examiner? A. Yes, of course.

Q. Are they all based on a general subject, one subject, we will say? A. There are a number of ramifications and, as I say, if you touch on one of these you always bring in this one. If one might use an analogy, if you touch an octopus on one tentacle all the others react. That shows that there is systemization of the material and that it is vague.

Q. Now, you spoke about him having some difficulty in his thinking operations. Just what difficulty did you find? A. I testified it was vague, that is to say, he is unable to present a logical statement about any aspect of his case in his present situation, and, secondly, his distractibility. I forgot to add that this distractibility is the result of internal things, not external things.

For example, if you and I were talking on some topic and somebody came in and yelled something, the noise of it might distract us from our present topic; that would be an outer distractibility, but his comes from within, and he has to be forcibly brought back to the topic at hand.

Q. Does this distractibility underlie this one idea of the theory of economics he has? A. That is mixed up in it. Its ramifications are such that I do not understand it, although I have tried to.

Q. Do you think his theories and ideas are superior to the average man's intelligence on the subject that he is talking about? A. I think he thinks they are, but there did not seem any way of proving it.

Q. What would be the norm on that? A. I don't know that one could conceive what is the norm on it; I can only say that I could not follow his argument on numerous occasions. Whether I believe in it or not has nothing to do with it. I couldn't follow it.

Q. Now, you say that you examined him again on February 6th or 7th. A. February 7th.

Q. Did you examine him alone or with others? A. With three other psychiatrists.

Q. You had the three with you at that time. What did that examination consist of? A. About the same thing.

Q. And that took about two hours? A. About two hours less the facts of the history because that was well-established.

Q. Do you think that there was any possibility during the two hours that you were talking with him that he might have been feigning in any way? A. Oh, no, I don't think so.

Q. You don't think that would have been possible? A. No, he was most cooperative.

Q. Was the examination on February 6th any different from the one on December 13th? A. Only as I said, I spent less time on the actual historical material with which we were acquainted at that time. It had to do with his present situation essentially.

Q. You think that Mr. Pound has delusions, did I understand you to say? A. Yes.

Q. And that has to do with self-importance? A. Yes.

Q. Any other delusions? A. I think he approaches quite clearly the delusional; he approaches the delusional in his vague schemes for the rehabilitation of the world. Most of us would be appalled by that task, but it does not seem to faze Mr. Pound.

Q. Do you think it is a delusion any different than some of these other European leaders had in that they had an idea they were going to conquer the world? A. I haven't had a chance to examine them.

Q. But what I am getting at is whether you think it might be similar? A. It might be, but I have never examined them.

Q. In connection with the charge of treason, did Mr. Pound discuss with you his activities in broadcasting? A. Yes, he told us about his broadcasts.

Q. And what did he say about that with respect to whether he thought that it was treason, or not? A. He said that it was not treason.

Q. Now, did the fact that he did not consider it treason have any bearing on the judgment which you formed in this connection? A. It would have this importance: it shows clearly that he was out of touch with a very large segment of the world, and it shows more clearly than anything else perhaps how his world was built for himself. You and I are living in what one is pleased to call the realities of the situation.

Q. Might it not be that he believed that he was not exactly legally liable for treason? A. If you will leave the word "legal" out I will agree with you.

Q. Wouldn't that be a matter which indicated that he was not of sound mind? A. Yes.

Q. Now, I think you answered the question that he understands, in your opinion, the charge he was under? A. Yes.

Q. And that he understood that he was brought over here to be tried for that charge? A. Yes.

Q. Now, will you explain to the jury why you do not think he is able to consult with counsel? A. Because I do not have any doubt but that his counsel would have the same experience I had with him, namely, that when he would try to pin him down to anything he would be left out on a limb just as I was time after time through his distractibility and vagueness.

Q. Do you think he does not realize he made these broadcasts? A. Oh, yes, he knows that.

Q. And that he did write the scripts from which he broadcast? A. I didn't ask him if he wrote them, but I presume he did.

Q. And did he tell you that he had turned over to the Government the manuscripts and scripts? A. He did not tell me.

Q. Did you ask him how many times, or how often he broadcast? A. That is a matter of record. I had the record on that.

Q. You did not think that that entered into the situation of whether he was able to consult with counsel? A. No.

Q. And in your opinion, as I understand it, the reason that it would be hard to confer with counsel is that it is hard to stay on a subject, is that right? A. It is hard to stay on a subject, and when you end up you don't finish with any coherent statement or intelligent thought.

Q. Well, he answered your questions? A. No, no, when I say, "Mr. Pound, you are out to defend the Constitution; now, that is a lengthy document, will you tell me what items are you out to defend specifically?", why, he will say "The President is a magistrate with delegated powers." That is all I could get on this question.

From then on he goes through all those ramifications about Confucius, and Heaven knows what.

Q. Doesn't he discuss the money and other clauses in the Constitution? A. Yes.

Q. And that would be reasonable evidence he knew how he is going to save the Constitution? A. By inference, but there isn't any clear statement, and then he goes on to these other things I have indicated which may play a part in the general scheme of things to him, but not to me.

Q. What do you think about his intelligence? A. That was investigated at length by the psychiatrists at the hospital. I do not remember the figure, but I think it is superior.

Q. You think he is superior in intelligence? A. Yes.

Mr. Cornell: Your Honor, I object to that. The other doctor is here, and to have this doctor testify would be hearsay.

By Mr. Matlack:

Q. What is your observation of his intelligence? A. I think it is not too high at the present time because of actual difficulties in his thinking processes.

Q. His memory, you say, is good though? A. Except for the period of the last summer, as far as I can make out.

Mr. Matlack: I think that is all, Doctor. Thank you, very much.

Mr. Cornell: May I ask a few more questions, if Your Honor please, in rebuttal?

The Court: All right.

Redirect Examination by Mr. Cornell:

Q. Doctor, Mr. Matlack questioned you about the length of that examination and about the investigations which you had made into Mr. Pound's history. I suppose you also had the record of the period he was under observation in the hospital, is that right? A. Yes.

Q. How long a period was that? A. I think it was around ten days in Gallinger Hospital.

Q. That was the first time, and what was the other? A. He has been in St. Elizabeths about two months.

Q. And all that time he was under psychiatric observation? A. Yes.

Q. So that you had the benefit not only of your examination but of the information gained by the other doctors in those two months? A. Yes.

Q. Now the Assistant Attorney General has questioned you somewhat concerning the effect of Mr. Pound's being a writer and also the fact that this is a treason indictment, and I am going to ask you a hypothetical question: Assuming that you knew nothing whatever about Mr. Pound being a poet, a man of some literary attainments, and assume that you knew nothing about his broadcasts over the Italian radio, and being charged with treason, and that he came in off the street and you questioned him as you did, would you, without knowing these special facts, be of the same opinion as to his ability to meet a charge against him? A. Yes, I would.

Q. In other words, then, it is not based on anything extraordinary you found about Mr. Pound? A. No.

Q. But his difficulty to follow through a certain chain of reasoning? A. Yes.

Q. Even assuming that you would not be able to put his mental illness in any particular classification, would you say that his inability to reason, and his distractibility would prevent a lawyer from adequately defending him? A. Yes, I would say that is the vital thing here. What we call it is for the purpose of our diagnosis.

Q. Now, Mr. Matlack questioned you about these delusions Mr. Pound has. I suppose you, or I, or others could have some one of them and it would not have any significance, but it is the accumulation of delusions along different lines which leads you to suspect a deranged condition here? A. Yes.

Q. You mentioned the word "systematization." Do you mean by that that he has a system of reasoning which is embedded in his mentality so that it is impossible for him to think outside of that system? A. Yes.

Q. Would it make it impossible for him to understand this charge made against him? A. I think it would be very difficult. I will go further and say impossible.

Q. I am not sure that this is a proper question, but do you think it would add anything to your description of him if we were to put him on the witness stand and question him concerning this case and see how he reacts? A. Well, I can only say I feel sure enough in my own mind that my opinion would be corroborated by everybody hearing him.

Q. Do you think you have been able to describe his present mental reactions so that it is not necessary to distress him by putting him on the stand? A. I would think so.

Mr. Cornell: That is all.

Recross Examination by Mr. Matlack:

Q. Do I understand you now to say that you base your opinion partly on some hospital records from the time you first examined him up to February 7th? A. Yes, sir.

Q. How much of your opinion is based on that? A. Nothing essential because they found the same things we did. It is a static picture so far as memory is concerned, and nothing startling was added. That is, what I term confabulation came out graphically in connection with his inability to think. He was grandiose and hard to talk to, and this second time he had more of that than when I saw him the first time.

Mr. Matlack: That is all, Doctor.

By the Court:

Q. Let me ask you a question, Doctor. You made a written report to me in conjunction with other psychiatrists under date of December 14th, did you not? A. Yes.

Q. Now, did each of the psychiatrists examine him separately, or did you have your examination together? A. No, all but about fifteen minutes was my own examination.

Q. I do not think it was brought out that your examination was in connection with Dr. Overholser of St. Elizabeths? A. Yes.

Q. And Dr. King of the Public Health Service? A. Yes.

Q. And Dr. Gilbert of Gallinger? A. Yes.

Q. And all four of you joined in that report to me and reached the same conclusion? A. Yes.

Q. And that was the same conclusion you arrived at? A. Yes, it was the same thing.

Q. There has been no disagreement at all? A. No.

The Court: That is all.

(Witness excused.)

Mr. Cornell: Call Dr. King.

Thereupon—Dr. Marion R. King was called as a witness for and on behalf of the Defendant, and being first duly sworn, was examined and testified as follows:

The Clerk of the Court: Be seated, please, and state your full name.

The Witness: My name is Marion R. King.

Direct Examination by Mr. Cornell:

Q. Dr. King, will you kindly state your official capacity at the present time? A. I am Medical Director of the United States Public Health Service, also of the Bureau of Prisons of the Department of Justice.

Q. Then you are the chief medical officer having to do with criminal matters insofar as the Government is concerned? A. Insofar as health, mental and physical health of prisoners of the Bureau of Prisons is concerned, yes, sir.

Q. Are you in charge of medical matters relating to all Federal prisoners? A. Yes, sir.

Q. How long have you held that position? A. Since September 1, 1922.

If you please, I would like to supplement that, that my connection with the Bureau of Prisons is in an adivsory capacity. I do not have complete charge of all matters of health or otherwise. It is under the supervision and direction of the Director of Prisons.

Q. Then what is your connection in the Public Health Service? A. In the office of Public Health Service of the Bureau of Prisons in charge of medical and psychiatric care of prisoners.

Q. Then you are associated with the Bureau of Prisons? A. Yes, my title is Medical Director.

Q. Medical Director of the Bureau of Prisons? A. Yes, and also of the Public Health Service.

Q. How long have you been with the Public Health Service? A. 26 years.

Q. Were you in private practice prior to that time? A. I was in the Medical Corps of the Army during the first war, First World War, and then in private practice for approximately 18 months, and then entered the Public Health Service.

Q. During your connection with the Public Health Service have you specialized in psychiatry? A. A great deal of it.

Q. Approximately at the present time how much of your time is taken up with psychiatric matters? A. Approximately 50 per cent.

Q. Where did you go to medical school? A. Stanford University.

Q. Did you have any postgraduate training? A. Yes.

Q. Are you the author of any works on psychiatric problems? A. Some articles dealing with mental health of the prisoners. I was instrumental in the development of physicians' treatment and study of borderline mental cases at Springfield, Missouri.

Q. Do you regard yourself as having special knowledge in the psychiatric field? A. Yes.

Q. Will you tell us on what occasions you have examined Mr. Pound, and what other investigations concerning him you have made? A. I examined the defendant on at least four occasions at Gallinger Hospital during December, 1945. Subsequently I examined him on one occasion alone at St. Elizabeths Hospital. That was January 29, 1946. And then jointly with three other physicians on February 7, 1946.

Q. Those other physicians are Dr. Muncie, Dr. Overholser, and Dr. Gilbert? A. Yes.

Q. The other three doctors who are here this morning, is that right? A. That is right.

Q. Did you also make any investigation of his previous life as revealed in his writings, for instance, or his own accounts of his earlier days? A. Yes, careful consideration was given to his life-long history, including his achievements and progress, and contact and dealings with others.

Q. How much have you read of his literary output? A. Very little of the poetry. I have seen one of the Cantos, and samples of poetry that have been reproduced from others.

Q. Have you read any of his economic tracts? A. Yes.

Q. And have you read the text of any of the broadcasts which it is said he made from Italy? A. Yes.

Q. Have you also had the benefit of records of psychiatric observation at Gallinger and St. Elizabeths Hospital? A. Yes, sir.

Q. How long a period did those records cover? A. From December 4, 1945.

Q. And to when did they run? A. To the date of the last examination.

Q. Now, from your examination of him, and investigation of records of observation in the hospitals, are you able to give an opinion as to whether Mr. Pound is possessed of sufficient mental capacity to understand and intelligently participate in the defense of the indictment here which charges him with treason? A. Yes.

Q. Can you give us your opinion, and also the reasoning on which it is based? A. After rather careful consideration of his life-long history, and especially his progress during the last few years, it is my opinion that he has always been a sensitive, eccentric, cynical person, and these characteristics have been accentuated in the last few years to such an extent that he is afflicted with a paranoid state of psychotic proportions which renders him unfit for trial.

Q. I presume a person can be psychotic, might even have paranoid tendencies, and be eccentric and cynical, and still be able to stand trial, is that true? A. Yes.

Q. What other considerations are there in his case which make him unable to stand trial, in your opinion? A. He has deviated from his chosen profession in that he has become preoccupied with economic and governmental problems to such an extent that during discussion of those problems he manifests such a sudden and such a marked feeling and tone that he reaches the point of exhaustion, and this unusual propensity, intense feeling, is quite characteristic of paranoid conditions and is sufficient, in my opinion, to permit, at least create, considerable confusion; at least that was the situation when I examined him, so that it is very difficult for him to explain his theories and proposals in a clear and concise logical manner.

He also exhibited considerable distractibility, easily distracted from the subject of the conversation, and it was difficult for him to come back to the point under discussion.

Q. Have you seen such symptoms as those in other men under accusation of crime, or men convicted of crime? A. I have seen many cases of this type not only among people who were charged with crime, or convicted of crime, but also among those who have not been charged with an offense.

Q. Do you regard this inability to reason properly, this condition of distractibility, as the major reason why it would be, in your opinion, impossible for him to stand trial? A. One of the major reasons.

Q. Did you discuss the actual nature of his case sufficiently to determine whether he is able to reason intelligently about it? A. Yes.

Q. And is he able to reason about it intelligently? A. No, not in a logical manner over a long period of time.

Q. In other words, he may be able to reason for a time, and then exhaustion and intense emotional disturbance would distract so that he cannot continue indefinitely, is that right? A. That is correct.

Q. Would you tell us who it was that asked you to make this examination in the first place? A. The Director of the Bureau of Prisons.

Q. That is Mr. Bennett? A. Yes.

Q. And do you know at whose instance Mr. Bennett asked you to make this examination? A. The Chief Justice of the District Court of the District of Columbia.

Q. That is Mr. Chief Justice Laws who is presiding here? A. Yes, sir.

Q. And I made no request of you as defense counsel to intervene in the case, did I? A. No.

Q. So that it was at a request coming from the Chief Justice of the District Court of the District of Columbia that you examined Mr. Pound? A. The request was made to Mr. Bennett and passed on.

Q. And previous to your first examination of Mr. Pound did you have any discussions with me about his case? A. No.

Q. I am going to ask you a question which I put to Dr. Muncie: Assume that Mr. Pound was not the unusual person that he is, and that he had not been charged with having committed the extraordinary crime he is charged with; assume that he was just another person under a charge for some petty offense, just a man in the street, would you have any different opinion about him in regard to his ability to undergo a criminal trial? A. In evaluating the mental condition of any defendant one must always consider culture, intelligence and other traits. I think that in this particular case, the superior intelligence, the choice professional field and the favorable progress in that particular activity are important factors, because the deviation from that field, the constant preoccupation with other activities are significant in this case.

Q. You spoke of personal history of the individual. A. This particular individual, yes.

Q. Then the fact that he is a great literary figure, and the fact that he is supposed to have committed treason, wouldn't enter into it? A. No.

Q. This emotion, exhaustion and inability to reason, would that make it difficult or impossible for Mr. Pound to go through the ordeal of a trial? A. Yes.

Q. If at the start he had some semblance of reason, do you think he would be able to keep that balance throughout the trial? A. I don't think he would, judging from my experience with him. In my observations during the examinations he became exhausted and intensely wrought up when discussing these problems which have a bearing on his case, to such an extent that on two or three occasions he almost reached the point of collapse, and I am quite convinced that that would be repeated under certain conditions, and I am sure a trial would involve that.

Q. If trial would subject him to the state you speak about, do you think that would bring on collapse? A. Yes.

Q. Do you mean physical or mental or both? A. Both. The physical would be induced by the intense emotional tension.

Q. Just one more question; you mentioned distractibility. Would you try to explain to the jury in what way his reasoning could be said to be distractible? What have you found in him that causes you to use that term? A. I found it was difficult for him to pursue a topic of conversation in a logical, reasonable and persistent manner. He gets sidetracked and talks about some other subject, possibly closely allied but not definitely connected.

Q. Was there any tendency when he got sidetracked to go off on the same track again? A. Yes.

Q. What does he usually get into? A. Usually the trend involves economic theories and proposals and much of it revolved about his revision of the monetary system.

Q. Then if you undertook to question him about his activities in Rome he would get off into this sidetrack on monetary theories? A. Yes.

Mr. Cornell: That is all.

Cross-Examination by Mr. Anderson:

Q. Doctor, if he got off on this sidetrack on a question could you get him to answer it again later? A. Yes.

Q. Could you get him to repeat it again when he would get side-tracked? A. Sometimes.

Q. Did you ask him about his life history? A. Yes.

Q. And did he tell you about his life history correctly as far as you could tell from the other records that you had? A. Yes.

Q. Did you ask him about his activities in Italy? A. Yes.

Q. During the course of the examination? A. Yes.

Q. And what did he tell you about those? A. He went to Italy about 1924. His health was not too good at that time. He submitted to two or three operations. I do not remember whether they were all carried out in Paris or whether it was finished in Italy, but he had been in Italy on those occasions.

He had studied the Romance languages, and was very much interested in Italian culture, and after that Italy was his principal headquarters.

He resided there, and as far as his own ability was concerned he did a lot of work in translating and investigating Oriental classics, and during that period, too, he was very much concerned with political, economic and monetary problems. He became preoccupied with such matters to such an extent that it interfered largely with his own profession, without any profit or gain incidentally. One point I think is significant, that he became so consumed with these other fields because he developed a belief that most government officials were tyrannical and it behooved him to do what he could to overcome that and safeguard the citizens' rights. Therefore, he wrote two pamphlets on economics and became very greatly concerned and interested in such matters.

As time went on his enthusiasm became greater, and there is no question but that he has a lot of sudden, emotional feeling in connection with these hobbies, or these special interests, so that during the time of examinations he constantly told me about these ideas and beliefs with all the energy of which he was capable, which indicated that these matters more or less dominated his life, dominated his feelings.

He was inclined to argue and discuss them almost to the point of exhaustion. That is all indicative of a paranoid condition. That is really the evidence, as I interpret the case, the evidence of mental illness. It is not a case of well balanced, well developed resentment, people usually have some hostility when their feelings are hurt or they imagine they have been discriminated against. Something of that kind occurs to average individuals almost every day. But here we have a case where something happened many years ago. For example, he told a story of being mistreated or abused by a minor consular official in Paris in 1940, and elaborated on that as an example of the tyranny of government officials. It may be very true that he was mistreated, but that is not sufficient justification for such a reaction.

As for the life and vocation in which he was proficient, his work was outstanding, but he became sidetracked, and thereafter appointed himself as guardian of the citizenry to abolish enmities of an international type.

Q. Did he tell you about his writing of manuscripts and making broadcasts during the war? A. Yes, sir.

Q. And from what he had told you did his answers and comments seem logical? A. No.

Q. And in what respect? A. His statements in that respect were usually vague, sometimes almost incoherent. It was difficult to ascertain his true motives because it was difficult for him to explain it and, incidentally, that was one of his worries, to have people understand him. He has a belief that he is misunderstood.

He implies that all his efforts, including his trip to the United States in 1939, and later his broadcasts, were carried out for the purpose of putting over these ideas and theories which he felt would bring about peace and order.

Now, another point I think is of significance here is this. I am convinced he glorifies in his rebelliousness rather than disguising it, and that again is indicative of a paranoid condition or paranoid state.

I think it is true, however, that some of his utterances, and maybe some of his output, is wilful, that it should be regarded as wilful, deliberate, and it might be classified as normal but, as I have indicated, I think much of it is indicative of a mental abnormality.

I think I should say it is impossible to sift out the absolute normal from the significant abnormal findings and facts, and in my judgment the latter predominate; that is to say, this paranoid state which now, to my mind, has been present for many, many years, has increased to such an extent that it has influenced his entire life, and through his own folly, and due to this defect, he has got himself into trouble more than once.

It is also significant, I think, that he has never hesitated, not only in these matters we are just talking about, but also problems that have been incident to his own person and profit, he has never hesitated to criticize, or vilify, or condemn others in no uncertain terms, even without provocation, without good cause, or without any cause. Without question he has been his own worst enemy in that respect.

Q. By profession he is a poet, isn't he? A. That's right, that is what I refer to.

Q. Have you read his poetry? A. Some of it.

Q. And have you read poetry by other poets? A. Some.

Q. And would the fact, if it is a fact, that you had some difficulty in understanding his poetry, would that have an effect in reaching your conclusion that poetry was not important to him, meaning the defendant? A. It is my conviction from what I have heard from others who are qualified in the field of poetry, which incidentally I am not, that his achievements have been outstanding in that particular field, and he has been very successful in that particular field.

Q. Do you know how old he is at the present time? A. He is 60 years old.

Q. Would his age have anything to do with his condition, in your opinion? A. No.

Q. I believe you stated you had examined him four times in 1945 and once in January, and once in February? A. That's right.

Q. Would you tell us briefly what type of examination you made at that time? A. I examined him alone for at least two hours duration, and attempted to follow a plan which is standard in conducting psychiatric examinations, and I found, after starting the examination, that I would have more information about the patient by permitting him to go ahead and talk. He chafes under cross-examination and restrictions, but does pretty well when allowed to proceed on his own accord; it is his own statement that he can explain his feelings and his ideas very much better if he is allowed to let the subject flow and not be interrupted too much.

Q. So the examinations were rather informal in that respect? A. As a matter of fact, he was permitted to recline on a bed when I examined him alone. That again was helpful in gaining me his cooperation because for a long period of time he had been accustomed to doing a lot of his work while reclining in bed, but in the joint examination with the others it was conducted in rather a formal manner in a room sitting in chairs.

Q. Did you make a physical examination? A. I did not personally, no.

Q. Was one made in your presence? A. No, sir.

Q. Do you know who made one? A. A physician at Gallinger Hospital, and I also understood at St. Elizabeths.

Q. In making your examination did you consider his life history, and the examination made at the hospital? A. Yes.

Q. Have you seen the report of the examination at the hospital, or know what it was? A. Yes.

Q. What was that? A. There was no serious condition, or serious disease or significant physical abnormality; nothing found that would affect his mental condition.

Q. Or his ability to stand trial? A. No.

Q. Would the fact that Mr. Pound is charged with treason in this case, would that have any greater bearing on his mental condition, more than if he was charged with any other crime? A. No.

Q. What classification would you state for Mr. Pound's mental condition according to your classifications pertaining to mental illness? A. I would say that would fall in the category of paranoid states, sometimes called paranoid conditions. That is not a very satisfactory term because it is part way between so-called paranoid schizophrenia or dementia praecox, paranoid type, and true paranoia. There are all types or gradations between the extremes, and it is my opinion that he falls in between those two extremes.

Q. Does he have a split personality? A. No.

Q. Just what is it that makes you place him in that category? A. He does not have the clear, well-defined systematized delusions of the paranoiac type; neither does he have the disassociation, the personal hallucinations or delusions, the disordered delusions that go with the dementia praecox, paranoid type, at the other extreme, but he does have a rather diffuse paranoid reaction which falls somewhere between those two fields, and that is the reason I would not classify him as a dementia praecox patient, or a case of true paranoia.

Q. In your opinion does he understand that he is charged with treason in this court? Does he know that that is what he is charged with? A. Yes, sir.

Q. And does he know the effect that that may have on him, that he must stand trial and may be acquitted or convicted? A. Yes, I think he understands that.

Q. Is he able to advise his attorney relative to the facts, the cause, and what he did? A. No, not in a reasonable manner.

Q. What do you mean by reasonable manner? A. I mean that he is so distractible, and has such a pressure of speech, and he becomes so excited that it is impossible to talk with him over a long period of time, or consult with him in a logical manner without him becoming completely exhausted.

Q. Well, if the attorney would take the lead, and if he could be able to divert his mind, do you think he would be able to aid in his defense? A. I don't think so. Judging from my conversations with him, he was unable to give you a clear view at all of his defense or his motives, his actions, or his operations in connection with his past activities.

Q. Does the fact that Mr. Pound might think that what he did was not treasonable have an effect in arriving at your opinion here? A. To a minor extent. I think he is devoid of the niceties of a true understanding of his condition. He does not believe he is a mentally sick person. He does not believe that he is guilty of a serious offense against the United States.

He believes that he is so superior, and so important, and has such information that he should be used as an agent of the United States.

He believes that he could be useful to this country if he were designated as a diplomat, or agent, and sent to Japan, for instance, or even to Russia, to deal with the people over there, with the idea now of maintaining the peace of the world, and then prior to the war he thinks he could have prevented the war because of this special information he claims to have.

Q. That could be a difference of opinion, could it not, Doctor? A. Yes; of course, that is my opinion.

Q. However, the fact that we differ would not affect his sanity or insanity, would it? A. I don't think a sane man in his status would make such a proposal.

Q. Do you think he is feigning insanity in any way? A. No.

Q. How much consideration did you give to his writings in arriving at your determination? A. To the extent that his writings on the monetary system, as far as I can ascertain, carried very little weight in this country, or elsewhere, although he had devoted a good deal of time to them. Over a period of many years he persisted in devoting too much time to matters of this type.

Q. Did you also consider his poetry in arriving at your conclusion? A. Yes.

Q. What consideration did you give to that? A. I concluded he was a very great poet because I read some of the opinions of experts in that field. That is not based on my particular evaluation of poetry because, as I indicated before, I am not qualified in that field.

Q. Are you qualified in the diplomatic field and economic field? A. No.

Q. And did what poetry you did read of his make good sense? A. I think what I read was all right.

Q. The fact that he may have had grandiose ideas, and a good idea of himself is not peculiar particularly? A. Not as to being a poet.

Q. And he is one of the leading poets of today? A. Yes.

Q. And not being able to follow argument, do you think that is a good reason for not being able to stand trial? A. That is one reason.

Q. What other reasons are there? A. In my opinion he is a mentally sick person.

Q. What is his intelligence; or what is his I. Q.? A. Very high.

Q. Do you know what it is? A. Something over 120. There has been no impairment of the intelligence over the years. That again is a characteristic of the disorder we are describing. Paranoids are very apt to develop among those of high intelligence whereas the schizophrenics are more likely to occur in individuals with low I. Q.

Q. By schizophrenic you mean a person with a split personality, do you not? A. Yes.

Q. That a person is a schizophrenic in and of itself does not mean that he is not able to stand trial? A. No, not at all. However, very early it was my impression that he should not be classified as a psychotic or insane person and, therefore, should not be absolved from the necessity of standing trial, but during subsequent examinations and interviews my view was changed because it became obvious, after talking to him for long periods of time, that much of his talk was definitely abnormal.

Q. It would make a difference, though, would it not, if any attorney, who was skilled in such matters, were attempting to get a direct answer from him rather than one who was not? A. I think so.

Q. Could you get a direct answer if you insisted on it? A. I don't know.

Q. Did you insist on a direct answer any time? A. Oh, yes.

Q. And did you get answers direct? A. Sometimes, yes.

Q. Did he tell you why he was brought over to the United States? A. Yes.

Q. What did he say? A. He declared that he had the feeling if he gave himself up and volunteered to come to this country that he would really be welcome because of the valuable information which he had which would be helpful in dealing with our enemies, but that after he was cast into confinement at Pisa he felt that he had been very definitely mistreated and double-crossed; and when he was brought to the United States he again felt that even though he came in the capacity of a prisoner, still and all there must be some way out so that he could divulge what he knew to the proper people. By the proper people he meant pretty high officials. He was willing to come for that reason. He felt that there were elements against him, perhaps commandos and British Secret Service, and even others involved in this double-cross proposition.

Q. Did he say when he first learned that he was charged with treason? A. I think it was while he was in Pisa.

Q. And why did he give himself up? What did he think he was charged with? What was the purpose of giving himself up? A. I don't know for sure, but I suppose he knew that he was to be apprehended as soon as possible. I don't know for sure.

Q. Do you know what he knew about that? A. No.

Q. Or when he knew he was charged with treason? A. No, I don't recall that.

Mr. Anderson: That is all.

Redirect Examination by Mr. Cornell:

Q. Doctor, you mentioned having read some of his poetry which seemed to you rational and poetic. A. I didn't pay much attention to it.

Q. Did you make any comparison between his early and late poetry in that respect? A. Well, I saw one of his poems, that he had prepared in the camp at Pisa which, of course, was incoherent and impossible for me to understand, as compared with the earlier.

Q. The poems you found coherent were earlier, is that right? A. Yes.

Q. During cross-examination you said that you considered his distractibility and deficiency in speech. Did you or the other doctors make any examination to determine if that same tendency was disclosed in his writing? Having in mind that he is a man of great literary ability, did you determine whether he was affected in his writing? A. Yes, he was, and he feels that due to fatigue and exhaustion that it would be impossible for him to write very much at the present time.

Q. In other words, he told you he could not write at the present time? A. That is right, and I believe it.

Q. Does the fact that he is a man of high intelligence have anything to do with his ability to understand and reason logically with regard to this offense? A. It would have if he were not afflicted with this paranoid reaction, but that is fixed to such an extent that he cannot reason in an intelligent manner.

Q. Being intelligent, then, does not help him? A. That is right.

Mr. Cornell: That is all.

Mr. Anderson: Doctor, just one question; a person may be abnormal along one line and yet be normal on other lines, might he not?

The Witness: He could have false ideas on one line, yes.

Mr. Anderson: That is all.

(Witness excused.)

Mr. Cornell: Call Dr. Overholser.

Thereupon—DR. WINFRED OVERHOLSER was called as a witness for and on behalf of the defendant, and being first duly sworn, was examined and testified as follows:

The Clerk of the Court: Be seated, please, and state your full name.

The Witness: My name is Winfred Overholser.

Direct Examination by Mr. Cornell:

Q. Dr. Overholser, will you tell me your profession at the present time? A. I am Superintendent of St. Elizabeths Hospital in this city.

Q. You are the chief medical officer of that hospital? A. Yes.

Q. What is the relation of that hospital to the United States Government? A. It is operated entirely by the Federal Government under the Federal Security Agency.

Q. Is there any other hospital in the District of Columbia which is a mental hospital? A. The psychiatric division of Gallinger Hospital.

Q. That is a division of the general hospital? A. Yes.

Q. Your hospital is purely mental? A. Yes.

Q. How many patients do you have? A. Just under seven thousand.

Q. How many doctors are directly serving under you? A. Approximately fifty, with some vacancies.

Q. How long have you been in charge of the institution? A. Since October, 1937.

Q. In what professional capacity were you engaged prior to that time? A. I was Commissioner of Mental Diseases in Massachusetts until December, 1936.

Q. Were you then chief medical officer of Massachusetts with reference to mental diseases? A. I was head of the department which administered ten hospitals.

Q. Prior to that? A. I had served in various capacities in the State hospital service from July, 1917, on, except some time I was in the Army Medical Corps.

Q. During all this time you have been connected with psychiatric work and public health, is that right? A. Psychiatric work, yes.

Q. How long have you been practicing medicine? A. I was graduated in 1916 from Chicago University.

Q. Are you the author of any text-books or scientific articles? A. Scientific articles.

Q. Will you tell us what examination you have made of Ezra Pound? A. I was requested to serve with Dr. King and Dr. Gilbert of Gallinger to advise the Chief Justice on the condition of the defendant after the defendant was committed to Gallinger Hospital for observation.

Q. The request came from Chief Justice Laws? A. Yes. I saw him on several occasions; I saw him alone twice, and I saw him with all of the other doctors at one date and another, and we made a report December 15, when we had Dr. Muncie with us in order that we might be talking about the same thing.

Q. What was your conclusion in that report? A. It was our opinion that the defendant was unfit mentally and unable to stand trial.

Q. And then since that date he has been in your hospital? A. He was admitted to St. Elizabeths on January 1, and has been there ever since.

Q. Has he been under constant observation? A. Yes, he has been under constant observation. I spent a long time in consultation with him and other doctors last Thursday, and I have before me the report made by the other physicians at the hospital, and I see no reason to change my opinion.

Q. Will you tell us the reasons which lead you to the conclusion that he is unable to participate in the trial of this indictment intelligently? A. Of course, in the first place we have the background of his history and the Department of Justice has been very helpful in making available what files they have concerning the case.

Q. Do you remember before that, or had you seen the text of his alleged broadcasts? A. Yes, and other things in addition. In the first place, it is quite obvious that the man has always been unusually eccentric through the years. He has undoubtedly a high regard of his own opinion, and has been extremely vituperative of those who disagree with him.

He has a very high degree of intelligence, there is no question on that score, and his relations with the world and other people during practically all his life have been those of a person who was very skeptical to say the least.

He is extremely free in his conversation; he has not been reticent by any stretch of the imagination, but his production has been unusually hard to follow. He speaks in bunches of ideas.

Q. You mean his production of speech? A. Yes, and rambling and illogical.

There was an episode shortly after he was taken into custody by the American forces in Italy during which he was extremely agitated and anxious, and he has shown episodes such as that sometimes when he was under observation both at Gallinger and St. Elizabeths. At times he has been extremely restless, and at times his speech has been more disconnected than others.

The ideas, perhaps, which he expresses indicate some of his views in connection with the war. In the first place, he is thoroughly convinced that if he had been allowed to send his messages to the Axis, which he wished to send, prior to 1940, there would have been no Axis even. In other words, that if given a free hand by those who were engaged in stultifying him, he could have prevented the war.

He lays a great deal of his difficulty at the door of British Secret Service, and other groups, which have opposed him.

He assures me, too, that he served a very useful purpose to the United States by remaining at the Italian prison camp to complete his translation of Confucius, which he regards as the greatest contribution to literature.

He is sure that he should not have been brought to this country in the capacity of a prisoner, but in the capacity of someone who was to be of great benefit to the United States in its post-war activities.

I might state that this constitutes a grandiosity of ideas and beliefs that goes far beyond the normal, even in a person who is as distraught in his mind as he is.

From a practical view of his advising with his attorney, there would be the fact that you cannot keep him on a straight line of conversation; he rambles around, and has such a naive grasp of the situation in which he finds himself, it would not be fair to him or his attorney to put him on trial.

Furthermore, due to the episode he had in Pisa when he was under confinement, I think there would be a much more violent reaction on top of this paranoid reaction if the trial was to proceed.

Q. You mentioned his naive reasoning. Will you expand on that? A. For example, he did not expect to be brought here. He did not expect to be put in prison when he got here. He thought he was double-crossed. He thought he was to be used by the government in any movement for the organization of the world. He is sure that his connections with Japan would enable him to deal with the delicate post-war situation. I think "naive" is a mild word to apply to that line of reasoning.

Q. Based upon your knowledge and understanding of the situation, how do you regard his ability to understand the situation and to answer questions in connection with the presentation of his defense? A. Well, with an infinite amount of patience, and an infinite amount of time, it might be possible sometime in the future to get a lucid answer to a question.

Q. In other words, would his discursiveness and inability to answer questions prevent his attorney from presenting his side of the picture in defense of this indictment? A. It would.

Mr. Cornell: Your witness.

The Court: Just a minute, I have to attend a meeting.

Members of the jury, do not talk to anyone about this case, and do not permit anyone to talk to you about it, and please do not discuss it among yourselves until I submit it to you. Be back at 2 o'clock.

Mr. Cornell: Your Honor, may Dr. Muncie be excused?

The Court: Yes, he may be excused.

(Thereupon, at 12:30 o'clock p.m., Court was recessed and further proceedings herein continued until 2 o'clock p.m., Wednesday, February 13, 1946.)

Afternoon Session

(Pursuant to recess heretofore taken, Court was reconvened at 2 o'clock p.m., Wednesday, February 13, 1946, and the following occurred:)

The Court: You may proceed.

Thereupon—Dr. Winfred Overholser, a witness heretofore called on behalf of the defendant, being recalled, and having been heretofore sworn, resumed the stand and testified further as follows: Cross-Examination by Mr. Matlack:

Q. Doctor, I understood you to say that you based your opinion partly on your own observation and partly on examination of records at the hospital. A. That is right.

Q. Do you have with you the records of the hospital showing his present condition? A. Yes, sir.

Q. Could you produce them? A. Surely; it is in my briefcase.

Q. Have you, yourself, treated Mr. Pound, or has that been left to your associates out there? A. Partly to the associates.

Q. Are these records the records made by the staff? A. That is right.

Q. And will you state by referring to them what the records show as to his present state of mental health? A. It is a rather bulky record, as you see.

Q. Can you summarize it? A. Essentially it is that there has been very little change in his condition since he came in. A summary of the case from the time he came in is pretty much in line with what I said this morning, and the whole staff has seen him. There has been some discussion about him which has not been formal; in fact, there has been no formal diagnosis they have made as yet.

Q. No formal diagnosis? A. No.

Q. What is your opinion as to the chances of improvement for this patient? A. As far as the basic sub-strata beneath these ideas of persecution, and so on, I should say not particularly good. The matter of the secondary "blow-up", so to speak, if I may use that slang expression, is not particularly important, and while he is in this particular condition I do not look for any fundamental change in his condition.

Q. By these blow-ups— A. These quiet states I think are more or less reaction to the stresses under which he may be placed. They are to my mind secondary. Fundamentally we are dealing with a paranoid condition, which I usually have found tends to progress rather than otherwise.

Q. Now, if he does not have these blow-ups, as you call them—I am going to use that expression, I think it is descriptive—where he is in those quiet states, would you say that during those periods he would be able to consult with counsel? A. No, I don't think so, not for the purposes of which we are speaking now.

Q. Now, what part does his background history play in your opinion as to his present sanity? A. It shows that we are dealing now with the end-product of an individual who throughout his lifetime has been highly antagonistic, highly eccentric, the whole world has revolved around him, he has been a querulous person, he has been less and less able to order his life. This has been a gradual evolution through his life, so that now we are dealing with the end-product, so to speak.

Q. Do you think that because he is eccentric that makes him unable to consult counsel? A. Oh, no.

Q. That is true of many people? A. Yes.

Q. That does not make him unable to consult with counsel? A. It might make him a nuisance.

Q. Make him a nuisance but not insane? A. Yes.

Q. I think you said one of the characteristics was that he was very vituperative to one who opposed his will? A. He has been.

Q. Do you think that, in itself, displays a person who could not be able to consult with counsel? A. Not in itself. I haven't said that any one of these things in itself would.

Q. I am going to come to that. I have forgotten what other thing you did say. I did understand you to say that he is vituperative, and eccentric; I don't know whether you used the word "sensitive" or not. A. No, but he is highly supersensitive.

Q. Now, couldn't a man who was eccentric, and vituperative, and all the other attributes that you have given to him rolled into one, still be able to consult with counsel? A. Even with all those three, and with nothing else, very likely, yes.

Q. I understand that what we are concerned with in this inquiry is not the question of the difference between right and wrong, that is, as to being able to distinguish between right and wrong, but whether he is able to consult with counsel and conduct a defense. A. That is correct.

Q. Did he give you in his general history anything about his belief in Fascism? A. I did not discuss that with him particularly.

> The Defendant: I never did believe in Fascism, God damn it; I am opposed to Fascism.

By Mr. Matlack:

Q. I don't know whether you answered the question, or not.

> The Court: I think he answered it.

By Mr. Matlack:

Q. Did he ever discuss with you his advocacy of Mussolini and his politics? A. In the most general terms. I didn't go into that in great detail, either. I looked upon that as a political matter.

Q. Well, that is what I am beginning to get at. Did you read his book entitled Jefferson and Mussolini? A. No.

Q. Did you take into consideration the fact that living in Italy, where the political philosophy was Fascism, that he may have become imbued with that philosophy?

Mr. Cornell: Your Honor, I object to this line of questioning and characterization of Mr. Pound, which I think is very distressing to him.

The Court: I will give you a certain latitude, but try not to disturb him if you can help it.

Mr. Matlack: I will strike the question and ask it again.

By Mr. Matlack:

Q. Did the fact that living in Italy, where Fascism was a political philosophy, and where most of the people in Italy had adopted the Mussolini Government, have any influence, do you think, on the question of whether he is sane or insane? A. No, I should not say so.

Q. Well, would the fact that somebody believed like Mussolini in his theories, or political philosophies, and the fact that others joined in his beliefs, and were otherwise normal, make them abnormal? A. I think that is a question of politics rather than psychiatry.

Q. Now, on the same theory, if somebody believes in an economic theory such as social credit, and is able to write and broadcast his theories about social credit, does the fact that he is imbued with a belief in social credit, if he is otherwise normal, make him abnormal or insane? A. I don't know that I mentioned his views on social credit. There are a great many people who take stock in that view of economics, but I do not think that because one believes in it stamps him any more than out of agreement with most people in this country at least.

Q. If I understand your testimony, he has certain grandiose ideas of saving the Constitution through the money clause in the Constitution, and that on certain economic theories if he could get to Japan he might have been of some service to the United States, and so on; I think that is what you testified to. A. I am not sure on the economic phase of the theories and, in fact, I never did get to the end of the explanation.

Q. Now, just how was he going to save the Constitution? A. There was some discussion about the money clause of the Constitution, but just what it had to do with saving the Constitution I was not quite clear.

Q. How does the fact that your conclusion is based on a paranoid state, if— A. I didn't say that; I couldn't get his explanation on that particular point.

Q. On what do you base your conclusion that he is in a paranoid state if it isn't based on his theories about saving the Constitution, and so on? A. The matter of his saving the Constitution, the mention about saving the Constitution is one of the factors. I don't remember that I mentioned that. I did mention particularly his idea that he could have prevented the formation of the Nazis; that he was the victim of machinations of the British Secret Service and antagonistic groups; that he was of far more use as an adviser to the Government than as a defendant in a criminal case.

Q. Did you ascertain what information he claimed to have that would be of such benefit to the Government? A. There was some discussion of it in an excursive and rambling way. I must say I was not impressed by the flow of the conversation. That is one of the reasons he asked us to—

Q. On the other hand, you think that under those circumstances, he thought he would be of service to the United States? A. As I say, he was unable to explain what that was, or how it would be accomplished. It was the fact he felt he was so important and of such value to the United States that I put him down as suffering a mental disorder.

Q. Did you talk to him at all about the charge of treason he is under? A. Yes.

Q. Did he understand that he had done anything treasonable? A. Apparently not, because he denied that he had done anything in connection with the Government of Italy against the United States. There was no significance apparently to that charge.

Q. Did he feel that because he did not think he had committed a treasonable act would make him an innocent man? A. No.

Q. Isn't it a fact that people charged with crime do that? A. Yes.

Q. And that doesn't make him innocent? A. No.

Q. Do you think he thought he understood what treason meant? A. I should say in a general way.

Q. Did he realize that he was subject to trial and possible conviction and punishment? A. I should say that his attitude was that the reasons for his being brought over as a prisoner was a part of the plot against him on the part of the British Secret Service and the Communist groups that he mentioned; in other words, that they were instigating the Department of Justice in the prosecution. That sounded to me pathological.

Q. Do you think that that could be without any foundation of fact when shortly before that he had given a statement to the Department as to his activities in which he recognized that he had been charged with treason? A. Oh, he knew he had been charged with treason. He told me that.

Q. And he knew it before he was brought to this country? A. Oh, yes.

Q. But did I understand you to say that notwithstanding that, that he thought he was coming over here to be of assistance to the United States in some other capacity? A. Yes.

Q. Do you think that that was something he might have told you out of whole cloth? A. It did not appear that way to me; taking into consideration the whole line of examination, I am quite convinced that there was no question of malingering.

Q. No malingering in that statement or any other, but in that particular statement you did not think that there was any question of malingering? A. No.

Q. Is your opinion based at all on the fact that the crime with which he is charged is closely tied up with his profession of writing? By that I mean the treason charge is the broadcasting and writing of manuscripts and broadcasting information to the United States, which is in line, that is, the written part of it is in line with his life's work? Do you base your opinion at all on the fact that he is charged with treason and that he has a psychosis, fear of apprehension? A. Will you please ask that again? Your question is not quite clear. You are asking whether this psychosis is due entirely to the fact that he is in this situation under indictment for a serious offense?

Q. That's right. A. No, I don't think so.

Q. You think that if he was not under arrest in a concentration camp or was, as he described, under arrest for treason, he would still have the same psychosis? A. He may not have believed it, possibly; those are secondary pretty much, but they are secondary.

Q. Do you think that he suffers from delusions of any kind? A. Yes.

Q. What delusions do you say he suffers from? A. Well, I think they are both delusions of grandeur and delusions of persecution, both of which are characteristic of what we call the paranoid condition.

Q. You don't say that he suffers with paranoia though? A. I will say it is a paranoid condition; the distinctions between paranoia, schizophrenia and one thing and another run into each other, but it resembles paranoia, if you wish to put it that way.

Q. Do you feel that he was so imbued with his economic theories, or whatever his message might have been, that even if he had realized the consequences of his treasonable act that he still would have broadcast? A. I haven't an opinion on it.

Mr. Matlack: I think that is all.
Mr. Cornell: I would like to ask a few more questions.

Redirect Examination by Mr. Cornell:

Q. Doctor, you said as to a number of specific delusions and specific deviations from the normal which you found in this case, that each one of those by itself would not necessarily indicate the opinion which you have given? A. Yes.

Q. However, would it not be true in any psychiatric investigation that one single instance of abnormality taken by itself would not indicate a conclusion one way or the other? A. Just as two lines do not make a picture.

Q. All must be considered together in order to arrive at a conclusion? A. That is correct.

Q. And when you do consider, not piecemeal but jointly, the points you have mentioned, your opinion is that the man suffers from the disease you described? A. That is correct.

Q. Would you say also, apart from your diagnosis, and apart from expressing any opinion with regard to sanity or insanity in the usual medical parlance, that the inability to understand and concentrate on the part of this individual was such that he could not participate in a trial? A. That is correct.

Q. So that all these eccentricities and abnormalities, and the medical diagnosis based on them, could be ignored, and still you would say because of the way this man reacts to questioning and reasoning, he still is unable to defend himself in this trial? A. These secondary situations standing by themselves would probably disqualify him from a proper trial, but I should prefer not even to segregate it the way you do, but to keep the whole picture.

Q. Perhaps this is a broad question to get an opinion on, but even if you were not determined in your mind as to the reasons which underlie the way in which he acts, would you not even then say that his reactions are such that he is not able to be tried, regardless of the diagnosis? A. I suppose my answer would be yes to that. It is a rather complicated question, and again I do not like to duck the other part.

Q. Suppose you put yourself in my place as an attorney questioning a man accused of a crime; I know nothing about psychiatric diagnosis any more than the average layman, and may not be able to form an opinion as to these abnormalities but, nevertheless, I know from questioning the man that I can't get an answer out of him. Putting yourself in the place of the layman would you be able to say whether this man is sufficiently able to reason and give coherent answers? A. I think he is not.

Q. And that would be apparent even to a layman who did not understand medical conditions which brought this about? A. I understand that it has been, and I certainly agree that it is the case.

Mr. Cornell: Thank you. That is all.

Redirect Examination by Mr. Matlack:

Q. But do I understand, Doctor, that you say he does have an understanding of the charge made against him, and an understanding of his position in relation thereto? A. He understands in the sense that he knows it is a fact that he has been indicted for certain actions which are of a serious criminal nature. I am not so sure I would say that he understands fully his relation thereto; that is, he knows what his name is, and he knows a person by that name has been indicted for that offense, but he has a significant lack of comprehension of all the events to comprehend fully the situation in which he now is, although intellectually he knows that there is such a thing as treason in acts against the United States.

Q. He has that information? A. He has an understanding intellectually which is different from appreciating his connection with that set of facts.

Q. Does he have any loss of memory as to the fact that he did write manuscripts and broadcast them? A. He speaks of that. His memory on some things is quite uncertain. There was some discussion, I remember, of him having dictated some manuscripts for broadcasts.

Q. But he understands what he did? A. In that sense, yes.

Q. Now, what is there about him that you say he cannot consult with his counsel when he understands the charge and understands what he did do? A. He understands the charge as far as applies to some abstract person. I do not think he comprehends or knows how that applies to this particular charge. That goes to his responsibility, and I am not discussing that, but I do say that his mental condition is such that he is unable to discuss with any degree of coherence the explanation for being in the situation in which he is, or his motive for so doing.

Q. Do you think his motivations and reasons for making the broadcasts have anything to do with his ability to tell his counsel what he did do? A. I should think so.

Q. Is it because of that fact that you think he is unfit to consult with counsel? A. Not wholly.

Q. Is it because you think anyone who has a paranoid state is unable to consult his counsel? A. Not necessarily. I think I have indicated that in a situation he might very readily have one of these, can I say "blow-ups", again, during which he would be quite unable perhaps to concentrate enough to recognize the importance of his defense.

Q. Of what duration are those blow-ups? A. Well, the one at Pisa lasted several weeks, as far as one can gather from the report of the psychiatrists there.

Q. What was this incident he told you happened at Pisa? I suppose he mentioned something to you. It has been mentioned here, and I think it should appear what it was, something he said? A. I have seen the reports of the psychiatrists.

Q. Do you pass on the reports of psychiatrists? A. No, not of those.

Q. What did Mr. Pound tell you? A. In the first place, he was quite sure then, as he tells it now, that lies were told on him specifically. It is quite likely that that was not the case, that he was in a state of panic, that he was off in his memory after that; he says he can't remember details clearly of what went on there even; that he developed some curious headaches and was determined at that time to be suffering from an anxiety neurosis state, and was given a little more latitude for that reason.

Q. Have you seen the opinion of those psychiatrists? A. Yes.

Q. What was that opinion? A. That he had anxiety neurosis.

Q. Could that have anything to do with the present opinion of the doctors around here?

> Mr. Cornell: I object to that.
>
> Mr. Matlack: He said he based it on their opinion.
>
> The Witness: I don't think it has a great deal to do with my opinion, but I was asked about what went on in Pisa, and I wasn't in Pisa myself.

By Mr. Matlack:

Q. You said you based it partly on reading those reports? A. Yes.

Q. And then I asked you did those doctors find him insane? A. They said he was not psychotic.

Q. That means he was not insane? A. They were, I think, interested in prison facts.

Q. When they said he was not psychotic that means he was not insane? A. That he was not suffering from a major mental disease. That was their impression. How long they saw him, I don't know, or what their experience was.

Q. Would you say that the incident known now as the Pisa incident was the result of one of these blow-ups? A. Yes. Apparently he had been held incommunicado in an uncovered cage of some kind out in the yard, and he apparently developed a neurotic state because of that.

Mr. Matlack: That is all.

Mr. Cornell: That is all.

Mr. Matlack: If the Court please, may Dr. Overholser be excused? Mr. Cornell says he has no objection.

The Court: Yes.

(Witness excused.)

Mr. Cornell: Will you call Dr. Gilbert?

Thereupon—DR. JOSEPH L. GILBERT, a witness called on behalf of the defendant, being first duly sworn, was examined and testified as follows:

The Clerk of the Court: Be seated, please, and state your full name.

The Witness: Dr. Joseph L. Gilbert.

Direct Examination by Mr. Cornell:

Q. Will you tell what your official position is at the present time? A. I am chief psychiatrist, Gallinger Municipal Hospital.

Q. That is in the District of Columbia? A. Washington, District of Columbia.

Q. And do you have charge of all the mental patients in that institution? A. I have charge of that department.

Q. Supervision of it? A. Yes.

Q. How long have you held this position? A. Fifteen years next April 1.

Q. During that time have you devoted yourself exclusively to psychiatry? A. Yes, and for some years before that.

Q. How many years have you specialized in that branch of medicine? A. I began my training in psychiatry in 1923, and then began to devote my entire time to psychiatry two years later, at the end of 1925, and entirely after January 1, 1926, on the staff of St. Elizabeths until April 1, 1931.

Q. How did you happen to become connected with this case? A. Well, Mr. Ezra Pound was admitted to the psychiatric department for mental observation December 3, 1945, and either shortly before or after the time of Mr. Pound's admission, I was directed by my superintendent, at the request of Dr. King of the Bureau of Prisons, Department of Justice, to join in the examination, I believe incident to a direction of this Court.

Q. And you and Dr. King and Dr. Overholser were jointly requested by the Court to make the examination, is that correct? A. That was my understanding, and I think through Dr. King.

Q. Now, when did you first examine Mr. Pound? Was it immediately upon his admission to your hospital? A. Not immediately. The first formal examination was on December 6, and then December 12 or December 13 formally, and at other times brief interviews during Mr. Pound's residence in the psychopathic department of Gallinger up to December 21.

Q. He was there, then, from December 3 to December 21? A. 1945.

Q. And you saw him regularly during that period? A. I saw him but not with any regularity, but at rather frequent intervals and on the dates specified for the purpose of formal examination.

Q. Did you also cause any investigation to be made by members of your staff during the times when he was not under your direct eye? A. We had some special examinations, not entirely special either, but some routine examinations made by some of the junior members of the staff, such as the taking of the blood plasm, a certain examination of the chest, and a special examination at my request of the genito-urinary system.

Q. Did you find any evidence from these physical examinations which would give any indication one way or the other as to his mental health? A. No, sir; the physical examinations were almost entirely negative, including X-rays, blood examination and genito-urinary examination.

Q. By "negative", do you mean they showed him to be normal in those respects? A. Relatively normal, yes, sir; no significant physical findings.

Q. After he left your hospital on December 21 did you have occasion to examine him further? A. Yes, sir; I examined him again, and the last time on February 7 at St. Elizabeths Hospital.

Q. Is that the only occasion since December 21 that you examined him? A. That's right.

Q. And that examination was in conjunction, was it, with the three doctors who have testified here? A. That's right.

Q. Now, will you tell us what your diagnosis was of his state based on your investigation? A. Yes, sir; as the result of my examinations of Mr. Pound during the period of observation in Gallinger, and on the date specified of the making of the examination of February 7, 1946, at St. Elizabeths Hospital, it is my opinion that Mr. Pound is of unsound mind and suffering from a paranoid state.

Q. Now, we are not very much more enlightened than we were before because I take it you will agree that these are not terms of great exactitude. I would like to have you tell us what things he exhibits of significance in this picture. A. Well, a paranoid state is not uncommon and is a well recognized mental disorder that is characterized in the beginning in a fair number of cases by what is known as the hypochondriacal stage of the disorder that may last for a longer or shorter period of time, usually rather prolonged, and during which the patient has a great many strange systemic symptoms, or symptoms referrable to the body, or any part of the body, and about which the person is concerned, and will inquire of the cause.

This period of illness may continue over several years, and following which the person moves into what is known as a persecutory state, or phase of the disease that may, not always, but may be characterized by delusions of persecution which may, in turn, be supplanted by delusions of grandeur, that is, delusions of self-importance, and the delusions of persecution may to some extent diminish, or the disorder may continue to be characterized by the delusions of persecution and delusions of grandeur, or delusions of self-importance. One or the other may be in preponderance, that is, one may overshadow the other, that is, the delusion of grandeur, or the delusions of persecution, and in some of the cases that are classified as paranoid states the disorder may subside for a considerable period of time, but more frequently remains a chronic type of mental disorder.

Q. You have been telling us what you mean by the term "paranoid" but not attempting to describe this particular individual, is that right? A. The major symptoms of a paranoid state or paranoid psychosis.

Q. That is what you have been giving? A. Yes.

Q. Now, did you find in this defendant the symptoms you mentioned of hypochondriasis and delusions of grandeur? A. Yes.

Q. Can you give us an illustration of how he is hypochondriac? A. On the various occasions of my examining him, when I have seen him he has complained that for at least four years he has felt unusually fatigued. He attempts to describe that condition by stating the work he has undertaken to attend to while reclining in bed. When those symptoms of fatigue are more marked he describes his feeling at the time as being unable to get flat enough in bed. During the various examinations he spoke of this fatigue and exhaustion very frequently, and more or less—I mean it was consistent, it was present all of the time he was interviewed, whether for a short or long period.

While he was in the psychiatric department of Gallinger he remained in bed practically all of the time with the possible exception of sitting up for his meals, or going to a bathroom nearby, and during long periods of interviews with him he remained reclining in bed, with the additional symptom of restlessness, rather rapid movements about the bed, and suddenly sitting or rising to the upright sitting position, or to move quickly about from the bed to a table nearby to get some paper, book or manuscript, and then to as suddenly throw himself on the bed and again assume the reclining position. This fatigue and exhaustion, which he states was completely reducing him, as he said, to the level of an imbecile in his thinking capacity, was notwithstanding the fact that he was undergoing no amount of physical activity. His thinking and mental activities were so greatly interfered with during the long or short periods of interviews that he easily, and a number of times during longer periods became quite exhausted, emotionally and physically, too.

Along with that was a certain amount of rather marked restlessness notwithstanding the reclining position in bed, and quick movements either into bed, or movements of experimentation, or movements to assume the sitting position, or movements to secure a book, a sheet of paper, or other articles in the room, in an agitated type of physical activity.

He spoke of his mental processes being in a fog, to use his own words. He admits during these periods of severe fatigue that he was unable to undertake temporarily any mental activity, and also complains of pressure throughout various regions of the head, which he describes as a feeling of hollowness, going through this gesture (indicating) with his fingers, describing the vortex of the skull, complaining that there was a feeling not only of pressure but of hollowness in that particular part of the cranium.

Q. Can you say whether in having him describe his symptoms and attitudes to you that there was any suspicion whatever of malingering, or did he appear to be entirely open and truthful about it? A. I did not feel that there was any element of conscious malingering in any of the symptoms that were expressed during my various examinations of him.

I have not so far gone into what might be called the purely psychiatric symptoms, but I did not feel that there was any conscious element of malingering.

Q. In other words, he may not himself have been testifying about his true physical condition, but the things he told you he actually believed to be true? A. Yes, I think that is correct.

Q. And can you tell us how he reacted to questioning about his predicament, about this indictment? Was he coherent and logical in his answers to questions, and his ability to understand the situation? A. Well, if I may qualify the answer a bit instead of answering yes or no.

Q. I do not want a yes or no answer. I would like to have you tell us what you found in your own way. A. When interrogating Mr. Pound for either short or long periods, it was exceedingly difficult to secure from him answers even to some of the simpler questions that were not rambling, occasionally irrelevant and extremely inconsistent. In other words, his answers, when obtained, and rather frequently answers were not obtained, to simple questions, his conversation was rambling and inconsistent, and at times very irrelevant.

Then, in fact, he would during his attempt to answer questions go into such rambling discourses on matters that had no relation to the question that he would lose the question and never get back to it, and even if I called him back to the question it was very frequently the case that you do not get a direct answer, or even any answer, that would be at all normal in certain phases, certain parts of the examination.

Then in addition there were at times rather marked outbursts, mental outbursts accompanied by profanity, not infrequently vulgarisms of one sort or another, with quite a strong tinge of hostility in certain phases of the examination that were at least inappropriate.

Q. Do you think that by reason of these reactions he would be able intelligently to consult with counsel sufficiently to defend against this indictment? A. I feel that by reason of his mental disorder, he is unable to consult intelligently with counsel to defend himself in any action pertaining to the present case.

Q. You mentioned a number of instances about his personality which are abnormal. Can you point to any particular indications which led you to that conclusion, or is it based on an over-all diagnosis? A. Yes, my conclusions are based on what I believe to be the presence of this not uncommon mental disorder, together with the abnormal additional content that I believe is present, leading to such extremely poor judgment that he would be unable to provide to counsel accurate or correct information that it would be necessary to give him at the time.

Q. Did you find, nevertheless, that he has an intellectual understanding of the nature of what he did, and of the fact that treason consists in certain violations? In other words, does he know what the law is, and does he recall his acts? A. I am sure that he recalls his acts very clearly, but it is my opinion that his motive, and motives for the act are of abnormal origin; in other words, resulting from abnormal thinking.

Q. Do you think he is able to judge his acts in relation to this crime with sufficient dispassion and freedom from those eccentric attitudes, so that he could put himself in the place of his counsel, or the jury, and to understand or be able to formulate his defense, or, on the other hand, are his acts so cloudy that he is unable to consider it with proper balance? A. I think the latter is true.

Q. Do you think that would prevent him from being able to stand trial under this indictment? A. Yes, to the degree, as I have stated, that he would be unable to cooperate in a defense, to cooperate and understand; nor could he cooperate, with the thinking that goes along with his various ideas, for his act or acts have been based on abnormal type of thinking away beyond what might be considered as a mistake or error, even mistake in judgment or error in judgment, far beyond that.

Mr. Cornell: Thank you, Doctor. You may examine.

Cross-Examination by Mr. Anderson:

Q. Dr. Gilbert, on these various occasions that you have mentioned on which you examined Mr. Pound, about how much time did you spend on each one of those? A. It would only be possible for me to estimate that roughly in hours, perhaps a total of somewhere between eight and twelve hours.

Q. And was that divided approximately equally according to the number of times? A. No, sir, some interviews were short, and then there were probably interviews not included in the eight to twelve hours when I saw him alone and not in conjunction with the other examiners.

Q. And, as I understand it, your opinion is based on your conversations with Mr. Pound and upon physical examinations that were made under your direction? A. Well, based on the history obtained, the mental symptoms that in my opinion are present, and that in my opinion also are not based on any physical disorder or physical phenomena, but in conjunction with which sufficient physical examination was made to determine fairly accurately his general physical condition.

Q. Did you talk with him with reference to his life history? A. Yes, sir.

Q. And did you also have documents or papers showing his life history, or information furnished from other sources to show his life history? A. Yes, I had that.

Q. And did the two correspond, or was there any difference in the two? A. Not any great difference in the factual data regarding his life history.

Q. He knew where he was born, in the State of Idaho, and when, and where he had resided, where he had gone to school, and the various places he had been without any trouble in recalling those matters? A. Well, I wouldn't say without any trouble, although I think he was fairly accurate in his statements in that regard.

During these various examinations that were conducted it would be necessary at times to discontinue the examinations for sometimes a short period, or sometimes a longer period, by reason of the exhaustion and fatigue of which I have spoken, and of which Mr. Pound complained and was, in my opinion, present to a rather extreme degree.

Q. Would his age have anything to do with his becoming exhausted? A. I believe not to the extent of which he complained. Furthermore, the physical examination failed to reveal, and it is my opinion that there are no serious physical handicaps; but for his sixty years, and slightly over, that he is in at least as good, if not better, physical condition than the average sixty-year-old. In other words, the fatigue and exhaustion of which he complains, as far as I could ascertain, were out of all proportion to any physical defects, which were only slight.

Q. And his mental intelligence is superior to the average individual of a like age, is it not? A. Yes, sir, or any other age.

Q. But it would not be superior to his mental intelligence at the time he was probably twenty-eight or thirty years of age, would it? A. His I. Q. was probably higher at a younger age, probably before the onset of this mental disorder.

Q. And what is his I. Q. at the present time? A. I did not do the formal psychological, but I am sure the one who did it is a very competent person, and it is something slightly over 120, if I remember correctly.

Q. Was it done at Gallinger Hospital under your charge and direction? A. Yes. Well, that is not exactly true. The psychologist who came was secured by Dr. King, through his service.

Q. I see. A. Of the Bureau of Prisons.

Q. But it was done in the regular, customary manner that you follow at the institution? A. Yes, sir, I am sure it was.

Q. You mentioned, I believe, Doctor, that Mr. Pound has grandiose ideas, and ideas of grandeur and ideas of persecution. Which is predominant in his case, if either is such? A. Well, I haven't gone into this very much in detail, but it was my belief that after completing my examination that the delusions of grandeur were perhaps somewhat more in the foreground than other abnormal types of thinking.

Q. And what are delusions of grandeur? A. Well, a delusion —I will have to break that up a little bit—is an idea not based on fact, not appropriate to the occasion, and not amenable to argument say, so a delusion of grandeur would be an idea of exaggerated importance, exaggerated self-esteem in his relation to the community, to the State, to the world. As in this particular case.

Q. In case of a great person thinking themselves as great, is that a delusion of grandeur? A. It may or may not be.

Q. And in case Mr. Pound thinks he is a great poet, would you say that is delusion of grandeur? A. No, I did not consider that as one of his delusions of grandeur.

Q. What did you consider? A. Well, his rather fixed belief that if certain circumstances had arisen that he would have been able to stop the formation of the so-called Axis and, therefore, have avoided the World War, and that if it had been possible for his writings to have reached the public, and especially important public officers throughout the world that the same thing would have happened, that the Axis would not have been formed, namely, the German-Italian-Japanese so-called Axis, and thereby the World War would have been prevented, and that there was a plot or conspiracy in certain quarters to prevent his writings from reaching the public, and especially certain important public officials he feels could have made use of his writings at the time and thereby have prevented the formation of the Axis and the World War; that he was interfered with in some way in setting up centers of learning where he also would have contributed to the prevention of the formation of the Axis and the World War; and that by his writings, his broadcasts, he was defending and saving the Constitution of the United States; that his economic theories were the last word in economy in the world, or in the economic field; that he believed he was being brought to America, after his imprisonment in Italy, for some use rather than—

Q. Rather than for trial? A. Rather than to face an indictment or trial; that on one trip he made back here in about 1939 he made efforts to contact certain important people, or leaders in Congress, and that his efforts to do so were interfered with, and that had he been able to make those contacts, and others, that all of this that has happened could have been prevented; that he believed he could have contributed to that by going to Moscow to see Mr. Stalin.

Q. You think then, Doctor, that he has a hypochondriacal condition or state, do you? A. Well, the medical diagnosis is paranoid state, in my opinion associated with the symptoms of delusions of grandeur more in the foreground than delusions of persecution, with the bodily symptoms, or so-called somatic symptoms, somatic meaning bodily, that I have described.

Q. Do you, or do you not, think that he has a hypochondriacal condition? A. Not alone. Hypochondriasis is one entity in medicine that is rather well recognized, and with the symptoms I have spoken of I used the term, hypochondriacal state to describe the paranoid state, or paranoid condition.

Q. In your opinion is his condition something that came on suddenly or came on over a period of years, or does it get progressively worse or get progressively better? A. Well, it is my opinion that it has been coming on for some years, and that the prognosis within the immediate future, or in a short period of time, is not favorable, that is, a recovery in a short period of time, in my opinion, is not to be expected.

Q. Did you discuss with Mr. Pound about how he lived in Italy, and what type of work he did, whether or not he wrote manuscripts, and if so what he did with them, and matters of that kind? A. Yes, he had lived for more than twenty years at Rapallo, Italy, where he said he had been doing writing and research of one sort or another during that period that he lived there, and also during a period of some years before that he lived in London, also in Paris, but for more than twenty years in Rapallo, Italy, with the exception of one or two trips, one at least, to America, to the United States, and other trips the details of which I do not recall.

Q. Did he mention the fact that he had made radio broadcasts or recordings? A. Yes, sir.

Q. And did he discuss all these matters clearly and intelligently? A. No, sir; as a matter of fact, it was exceedingly difficult, if not impossible, to get from him anything approaching coherent or clear or concise answers about any of his activities, except to listen to his conversations, to the discourses I have described previously as rambling and not infrequently irrelevant, to try to pick out from that the essence in the form of factual data.

Q. Did Mr. Pound know he was charged with treason at the time you talked with him? A. Yes, I am sure he did.

Q. Do you know when he first knew that? A. No.

Q. Did he tell you whether or not anyone told him the purpose of coming to this country? A. He may have said that he was told, but I do not recall his statement.

Q. Do you know where he got the basis for the belief that he was coming here to help the Government that you mentioned previously in your testimony? A. Well, his belief regarding helping the Government goes back over a period of at least a few years when he believed he was defending and saving the Constitution by his broadcasts.

Q. Pardon me, Doctor, was your testimony to the effect that he was coming to the United States at this time in order to help the Government, or did I misunderstand. A. He told me he believed he was being brought back to the United States, and I indicated that he thought he was coming back for some useful purpose rather than to face an indictment.

Q. And did he tell you where he got that belief? A. No, sir.

Q. You don't know whether someone may have told him that for the purpose of making him an easy prisoner, do you? A. No, sir, I do not, but I do not believe that is the case. I believe it is the outgrowth of his abnormal thinking.

Q. And do you believe he is able to comprehend what may be the outcome of a treason trial, should he be tried for treason? A.

To comprehend, yes, in a rather uncertain way he knows perhaps what would happen in case of his conviction on the charge.

Q. What causes you to believe he does in an uncertain way? Just what do you mean by that? A. Well, in the first place he told me he thought he was being brought back so he could be made some use of, and during one of my earliest interviews with him he stated that he believed he was worth more to the country alive than dead.

Q. Did he say why? A. Yes, at various times, and in a spotty manner, indicating that his knowledge of economic theories, of which he indicated he knew more than anyone else in the world, if they were applied to the world-wide situation even before the war or since.

Q. That could be a debatable question, could it not? A. Well, as a principle it could well be a debatable question, but in the case of Mr. Pound, to my way of thinking, and according to my examination, it was my opinion that it was a delusion of grandeur.

Q. He also thought that he had not committed treason because under the Constitution he was granted the right of free speech? A. Yes.

Q. Wouldn't that be a very good matter to present as a defense, or a possible defense? A. I don't know, you are taking me into legal fields, now.

Mr. Cornell: Your Honor, I object to that. The witness isn't qualified to answer that.

The Court: I think that is probably correct.

By Mr. Anderson:

Q. In your opinion, Doctor, do you think he is entirely incompetent to consult counsel and properly, rationally give information to prepare his defense in this case? A. I believe he is incompetent to do so.

Q. And you base your opinion upon what you have heretofore told us, do you, and also upon reading some of his works and writings? A. Well, I based my opinion on the examination of the case. It is true I have seen some of his writings.

Q. Is it possible to reach an opinion in a matter of this kind with any degree of certainty, or is it more or less a question of various individuals reaching a different conclusion on the same set of facts? A. That is rather involved, and I am afraid I might have to speak for others there, but for myself I am not at all uncertain of my opinion in this case.

Mr. Anderson: I think that is all, Doctor.

Mr. Cornell: That is all.

(Witness excused.)

Mr. Cornell: I rest, Your Honor.

Mr. Matlack: May we approach the bench?

The Court: Yes.

(Thereupon counsel approached the Court's bench and, out of the hearing of the jury, the following occurred):

Mr. Matlack: You are not going to call Pound?

Mr. Cornell: I don't think so.

Mr. Matlack: I was going to ask the Court to call him as the Court's witness.

The Court: I don't think so. If we call him he will take two or three hours. I do not think it is necessary. The Court of Appeals says very plainly you cannot disregard an opinion of the psychiatrists.

Mr. Cornell: I am afraid he might blow up. He has been pretty nervous.

The Court: You don't want to argue the case, do you?

Mr. Cornell: No.

Mr. Matlack: No.

(Thereupon counsel retired to the trial table and, in the hearing of the jury, the following occurred):

Mr. Cornell: I intend to make a motion for a directed verdict.

The Court: I will take the verdict, and so just for the record I will overrule it and note an exception.

COURT'S CHARGE TO THE JURY

The Court: Members of the Jury, there is a provision of our code in the laws of the District of Columbia to the effect that whenever a person is indicted for an offense, and before trial evidence is submitted to the judge that the accused is then insane the judge may cause a jury to be impanelled to inquire into the sanity or insanity of the accused, and if the jury shall find the accused to be then insane the Court may then bring about a commitment of the defendant to hospitalization, to remain in hospitalization until or unless there comes a time when it is found that he has recovered from his mental difficulties, and in that event he is certified back into the court for trial.

The reason for that law, of course, is obvious to all of us I am sure. It is absolutely essential that any person accused of the commission of a crime must be in a position to cooperate with counsel who is to defend him. He must understand the nature of the charges and be familiar and able to understand the offense which was alleged in the charge against him, to be able to tell the names of witnesses, what they might be able to say, and be able to give his own version of these acts which are alleged against him.

It is important, also, of course, that in the trial of the case that he be in position to cooperate with his counsel in his defense and, if he sees fit, if he chooses to take the stand, to testify understandingly and intelligently with regard to the facts in the case and to be cross-examined by the prosecution with regard to those facts and, of course, the law is humane to the extent that it does not want to bring about a person's breakdown at the trial of a criminal case if he is mentally ill and not able to stand the stress of a criminal trial.

In this particular case the defendant is charged with a serious offense, the offense of treason which, under certain conditions might result, if he is found guilty, in his punishment by electrocution, and when he was arraigned in court there was some suggestion made to me as the presiding judge that he was having mental difficulty, and on the strength of the showing that was then made, and later made in the form of affidavits, I committed him to Gallinger Hospital for examination.

It has been testified to before you correctly that we brought him to the point of having him examined by psychiatrists and physicians on mental diseases; we brought Dr. Overholser, who is the head of St. Elizabeths Hospital, one of the outstanding institutions of the United States, and run by the United States, and we brought to examine him also Dr. King who, as you have been told on the witness stand, holds a responsible position in the Public Health Service which attends to the mental as well as the physical condition of persons in the penal institutions throughout the United States. We brought into consultation also Dr. Gilbert, who is the head of the Division of Psychiatry at Gallinger Hospital, with which I think you are doubtless familiar. Then there was permitted to examine him at the request of Mr. Cornell, who appeared for Mr. Pound, Dr. Muncie, who is a leading psychiatrist, and I think the head of the department at Johns Hopkins University. You heard his qualifications.

Those doctors, after consultation, filed a written certificate with the Court indicating their unanimous view that Mr. Pound under his present state of mind was not in position to stand a trial, to cooperate with his counsel, and go through with a serious charge of this nature.

Government counsel have cooperated very readily in the investigation and were very fair in the entire situation and they, feeling that the code of law which I have explained to you should be complied with, filed in this court a motion that a jury be impanelled to pass upon this proposition. I agreed with the view of Government counsel that a jury be impanelled to look into it notwithstanding the unanimous opinion of these psychiatrists, and that is the reason why you have been impanelled today to hear the whole story, and those physicians have been questioned before you fully with regard to the situation.

It therefore becomes your duty now to advise me whether in your judgment you find that Mr. Pound is in position to cooperate with his counsel, to stand trial without causing him to crack up or break down; whether he is able to testify, if he sees fit, at the trial, to stand cross-examination, and in that regard, of course, you have heard the testimony of all these physicians on the subject, and there is no testimony to the contrary and, of course, these are men who have given a large part of their professional careers to the study of matters of this sort, who have been brought here for your guidance.

Under the state of the law you are not necessarily bound by what they say; you can disregard what they say and bring in a different verdict, but in a case of this type where the Government and the defense representatives have united in a clear and unequivocal view with regard to the situation, I presume you will have no difficulty in making up your mind. However it is my duty as the judge that whenever an issue is submitted to a jury to say to the jury that you are the sole judges of the facts so when you retire to the jury room now select a foreman and try to make up your minds whether this defendant is presently of unsound mind and when you make up your minds you answer the questions that the clerk will submit to you, and if you find that he is not of unsound mind you will return that kind of verdict.

Anything further?

Mr. Cornell: I think they should not draw any unfavorable inference from the fact that Mr. Pound did not take the stand.

The Court: Counsel asked me with regard to that and I advised with them that I did not think it was necessary for him to take the stand, so you will not draw any unfavorable inference from that.

(The jury retired and returned after three minutes.)

The Clerk of the Court: Mr. Foreman, has the jury agreed upon its verdict?

The Foreman of the Jury: It has.

The Clerk of the Court: What say you as to the respondent Ezra Pound? Is he of sound or unsound mind?

The Foreman of the Jury: Unsound mind.

The Clerk of the Court: Members of the jury, your foreman says you find the respondent Ezra Pound of unsound mind, and that is your verdict so say you each and all?

(All members of the jury indicated in the affirmative.)

(Thereupon, the hearing was concluded.)

ACKNOWLEDGMENTS

GRATEFUL ACKNOWLEDGMENT IS GIVEN to the following for permission to use their copyrighted material or literary property or other kindness to the author:

To Dorothy Shakespear Pound as Committee for Ezra Pound, incompetent, appointed by the District Court of the United States for the District of Columbia, for permission to print broadcasts by Ezra Pound at pages 1, 139, and 141; letter to Shakespear and Parkyn at page 7; lines from "The Pisan Cantos" at page 33; and a series of letters from Ezra Pound to Julien Cornell at pages 71-109.

To Dorothy Shakespear Pound individually for permission to print four letters from her to Julien Cornell appearing at pages 51, 53, 59, and 67. Thanks are also given to Mrs. Pound for her kindness in reading and correcting the manuscript of this book.

To Arthur V. Moore for permission to print his letter to James Laughlin at page 4, and his letter to Julien Cornell at page 49.

To Mrs. Valerie Eliot for permission to print the late T. S. Eliot's letter to Julien Cornell (copyright by Valerie Eliot) appearing at page 110. Mrs. Eliot was also kind enough to read and correct the portion of the manuscript in which her husband is mentioned.

To Leonie Adams for permission to print her letter to Julien Cornell appearing at page 116, and for her kindness in reading and correcting the portion of the manuscript relating to the award to Ezra Pound of the Bollingen Prize by the Library of Congress.

To Dr. Dale C. Cameron, Superintendent of Saint Elizabeths Hospital, and to Mrs. Dorothy S. Overholser for permission to print a letter from the late Dr. Winfred Overholser, former Superintendent of Saint Elizabeths, to Julien Cornell appearing at page 110.

To Thurman Arnold and to his publishers, Harcourt, Brace & World, Inc. for permission to print the quotation from his book *Fair Fights and Foul* appearing at page 67. Thanks are also given to Mr. Arnold for his courtesy in reading the portion of the manuscript dealing with the dismissal of the indictment.

To The New York Times for use of articles from its issues of November 7, 1945, March 14, 1946 and April 19, 1958 appearing at pages 12, 112, and 135; copyright 1945, 1946, and 1958, respectively, by The New York Times Company. Reprinted by permission.

To the New York Herald Tribune for permission to print articles from its issues of November 28, 1945, December 22, 1945, and February 14, 1946 by Robert E. Nichols and from its issue of February 21, 1949 by Carl Levin, appearing in this book at pages 24, 37, 44, and 119.

To The Saturday Review and to Bennett Cerf for permission to print a portion of his column "Trade Winds" in the March 16, 1946 issue of The Saturday Review, which appears at page 114 of this book.

To Life Magazine for its courtesy in granting permission to print an editorial entitled "An Artist Confined" (copyright 1956 by Time, Inc.) from the February 6, 1956 issue of Life Magazine, which appears at page 121.